As a physician, I find the experiential evidence Doug presents of significant and persistent life change after deliverance particularly impactful. Doug calls us to close the reality gap between what we perceive and what is possible through Jesus as Kingdom people so that we live in transformational faith rather than cognitive-only religiosity. A must-read for anyone who dares to be spurred on to operate in the power and authority that Jesus still gives us today.

—Lisa Burchett
Medical doctor

Very few people understand the connections between discipleship, healing, and deliverance. Doug carefully lays out those connections, allowing the readers to see them clearly. Discipleship, in a biblical sense, cannot prevail without healing and deliverance. Growing up in the full measure of Christ must involve the transformational work of the Holy Spirit who heals and delivers. This is vital. It is not only a prophecy. It is a promise.

—Rev. Genghis Chan
Chair, Canadian Chinese Alliance Churches Association

Light Up the Dark pulls back the curtains and shines a light on the vital role of deliverance in the church and spiritual formation. An informative, inspiring, and practical book, Doug Balzer shares stories of those who have found freedom and his heart for the church to reclaim deliverance as a normal part of discipleship. If deliverance is new to you, grab this book and discover the light of Jesus waiting to break through in a brand new way, it will change everything.

—Rev. Kirk D Cowman
Lead Pastor, Living Hope Alliance Church
Regina, Saskatchewan

This book captures the place of healing and deliverance in offering the gospel message. In a most compelling way, Doug clearly shows how the Holy Spirit brings power to the message. As a psychotherapist, I was captured by Doug's ability to bring clarity to the unity of mind and soul as lives are changed and disciples made through the Spirit's power. As in ancient times, this book displays how healing and deliverance continue to be available to all believers today as the gospel is presented and validated through changed lives.

—**Gerald L. Dahl, PhD (Hon)**
President, Strategic Team-Makers, Inc.
Board Certified Psychotherapist

Doug writes as a theologian, historian, academician, practitioner, and most importantly, as a transformed disciple who has been deeply impacted by inner healing and deliverance. Doug calls the church back to its role in God's restoration project, restoring deliverance and healing ministries to the church. I encourage all those who have a shared passion to see the church awakened and empowered by the Holy Spirit to bring people from the kingdom of darkness into the kingdom of light to read this book.

—**Ingrid Davis, D.Min.**
Leadership Coaching International

There are a plethora of books on disciple-making but few of them treat healing and deliverance as core to that practice. Doug's book addresses that much-overlooked need. His cogent findings from scripture, history, and research are comprehensive and compelling. I offer a high five for *Light Up the Dark*.

—**Roger Helland, D.Min.**
Prayer Ambassador, Evangelical Fellowship of Canada
Author of *The Devout Life*, *Missional Spirituality*
and *Magnificent Surrender*

Reclaiming the ministry of divine healing and particularly the ministry of deliverance is key for the postmodern Church as believer and non-believer alike increasingly recognize the spiritual and supernatural backdrop of life. Doug Balzer provides a timely and insightful book to help pastors, lay leaders, and the Church rediscover its ancient authority and voice for seeing people healed and set free. It's time for the North American Church to move again in the grace of God's power—this is a book that helps pave the way.

—Rev. Shane Gould
Lead Pastor, Wellspring Church
Burlington, Ontario

Doug challenges the church to reclaim the supernatural intervention of God to set people free from physical, emotional, and spiritual bondage and embrace this as a normal part of disciple-making. For far too long, healing and deliverance have been consigned to the shadows of our spiritual heritage and the church has been crippled by its indifference. With prophetic longing, Doug rekindles the appetite for healing and deliverance in the church and to impart a flame, dare I say, an unquenchable blaze, in the hearts of the next generation.

—Rev. David Hearn, D.Min.
Chair, Evangelical Fellowship of Canada
President, Christian & Missionary Alliance in Canada

Balzer correctly argues for collaboration among spiritual, psychological, and physical health practitioners in holistically serving the needs of the people they serve. I therefore encourage others to read this book and use its content for greater discussion and exploration of how individuals can be delivered more intimately into the presence of Christ and his healing power.

—Heather Heywood
Registered Psychologist

Dr. Doug Balzer's insightful and valuable book does indeed light up the darkness. Both balanced and biblical, Doug tackles questions and controversies over the realities of healing and deliverance ministry by integrating solid academic research, medicine, psychology, biblical study, real-life anecdotes, and testimonies of God's healing power and deliverance. Dr. Balzer sums it up best in his words: "Jesus and His gospel are way better than we know."

—**Paul L. King, Th.D., D.Min.**
Paul King Ministries

In a pluralistic, syncretistic society where all deities are considered equal, only the unequal display of Jesus's power will convince people of the supremacy of Christ. Doug has written a book that can help Christians access God's empowerment for accomplishing the mission of God. We desperately need Jesus's presence and power to turn around the downward trends of the church in the West.

—**Rob Reimer, D.Min**
Renewal Ministries International
Author of *Soul Care* and *Spiritual Authority*

In a society haunted by the supernatural, the church ironically needs to catch up by returning again to the supernaturally dependent discipleship of the early church. Balzer argues that ministries of healing and deliverance are the gospel experienced and are critical components of basic discipleship. This is a book that should be read by all non-charismatics who are interested in deepening their walk with Jesus and gaining credibility within a skeptical world. This book points to the antidote to the secularization of Christianity.

—**David John Seel, Jr., Ph.D.**
Cultural analyst and author of *The New
Copernicans: Millennials and the Survival of the Church*

Through some original research and interviews, Dr. Doug Balzer has created a profitable resource from well-regarded leaders of their narratives of breaking free from old patterns, voices, etc. These narratives and testimonies strengthen his original doctoral research and defense of this necessary topic. I've known Doug for three decades and watched him progress from a student to a doctor of the church to a published author. God has used Doug and his wife Teri to assist countless leaders to find freedom in their own lives and souls around the world. I commend this book to you.

—**Martin Sanders, D.Min.**
President & Founder of Global Leadership Inc
Director of Doctorate of Ministry Program
at Alliance Theological Seminary

Balzer makes an overwhelmingly compelling case for the restoration of healing and deliverance that only Jesus can do through his followers. This book not only answers the questions of the skeptic but also inspires the seeker that these experiential dimensions of Jesus's ministry are available now.

—**Robert S. Snow, Ph.D.**
Associate Professor of New Testament, Ambrose University

Doug Balzer takes us into zones which for many are discomforting, as he reminds the reader that healing and deliverance from evil influence are at the heart of the gospel. I invite you to read this book and be reminded how Christ is so utterly freeing and transforming. *Light Up the Dark* is instructive, inspirational, and rooted in the biblical narrative.

—**Brian C Stiller, D.Min.**
Global Ambassador, World Evangelical Alliance

LIGHT
UP THE
DARK

Restoring Healing and
Deliverance to Disciple Making

Douglas A. Balzer

Print ISBN: 978-1-4866-2184-2
eBook ISBN: 978-1-4866-2185-9

Word Alive Press
119 De Baets Street, Winnipeg, MB R2J 3R9
www.wordalivepress.ca

WORD ALIVE
—P R E S S—

Cataloguing in Publication may be obtained through Library and Archives Canada

Dedicated to Teri.

*My life partner for 30 years, who prayerfully,
patiently, and persistently sought and awaited my freedom.
Although twenty years ahead of me on these matters,
she walks together as one.*

CONTENTS

FOREWORD

BY DR. ROB REIMER

The Kingdom of God is the central message of Jesus. It is the first thing Jesus talks about: *"Repent, for the kingdom of heaven has come near"* (Matthew 4:17). It is the last thing Jesus teaches his disciples (Acts 1:3). Everywhere Jesus goes, he preaches about the kingdom and demonstrates its arrival with power. Therefore, it seems important that we should be able to quickly articulate what the Kingdom of God is all about.

The Kingdom of God is the reversal of everything that went wrong with the world when sin entered the world; it is the restoration of the way things were supposed to be. When sin entered the world, sickness entered the world. There wasn't any sickness before sin, and there won't be any sickness in heaven. When sin entered the world, demonization entered the world. There weren't any demonized people before sin entered the world and there won't be any demonized people in heaven. So, when Jesus preaches the Gospel of the kingdom, he heals the sick, casts out demons, saves the lost, and sets the captives free. He proclaimed the coming of the kingdom and then demonstrated it with power by overthrowing Satan's tyrannical rule.

Jesus doesn't just preach and demonstrate the Gospel of the kingdom; he empowers his disciples to do the same work (Matthew

10:1). He gives them authority to preach the Gospel of the kingdom and to drive out demons and heal the sick.

In the New Testament, there is no authentic proclamation of the Gospel of the kingdom without a demonstration of power. Jesus came to destroy the devil's works (1 John 3:8). In Mark 2, Jesus encounters a paralyzed man while he is preaching. His friends lower the man through the roof to see Jesus. Jesus says to him, *"Son, your sins are forgiven"* (Mark 2:5). Of course, this isn't really why the man came; he is paralyzed. It is obvious that he came to be healed by this well-known miracle worker. But I suspect that at least part of the reason why Jesus proclaimed him to be forgiven is because of the response it elicits from the religious leaders. The teachers of the law think to themselves, *"Who does this guy think he is? He can't proclaim forgiveness. That's blasphemy."* Jesus knows their thoughts and uses it as an opportunity to confront them. Jesus says, *"Which is easier: to say to this paralyzed man, 'Your sins are forgiven' or to say, 'Get up, take your mat and walk'? But I want you to know that the Son of Man has authority on earth to forgive sins"* (Mark 2:9-10). So, Jesus told the guy to take his mat and go home, and the man does just that to the amazement of the crowd.

It is a compelling story, but don't miss Jesus's logic. The proof that Jesus has authority to forgive sins is the power that Jesus demonstrates over the effects of sin. Sickness and demonization are the effects of a sin-stained planet. If Jesus is indeed the king who overcame sin, then he must be able to demonstrate that he has power over the effects of sin. If he has conquered sin, he must have power to overcome all the consequences of sin.

Some, of course, will object, 'yes, but that's Jesus; this isn't for everyone.' But this isn't just true for Jesus. In Matthew 10, Jesus sends his disciples out with authority to advance the kingdom. In Matthew 17, Jesus is up on the Mount of Transfiguration with Peter, James and John. The other disciples are down below doing ministry; they run into a young boy who has demons, but they can't get the boy free. Jesus returns and the desperate father runs up to Jesus and pleads with him for help; he tells Jesus that the disciples could not heal his son. Jesus turns to the disciples and says, *"You unbelieving and perverse generation... how long shall I stay with you? How long shall I put up with you?"* (Matthew 17:17). Jesus heals the boy, of course, but I want us to carefully observe Jesus's rebuke to his disciples. He called them 'unbelieving and perverse.' In the original language, this word, perverse, means to distort the truth. They were proclaiming the Gospel of the kingdom; they were preaching that the King had come to destroy the devil's works and set the captives free. But they could not demonstrate the message that they were proclaiming, and Jesus says that their lack of power, due to their unbelief, was a distortion of the Gospel of the kingdom. It was perverting the truth that they proclaimed. If we proclaim that, indeed, Jesus has overcome sin, we must be able to prove that by demonstrating Jesus's victory over the effects of sin.

I grew up in an Evangelical church where we believed the Bible was God's Word. But we didn't see healing or deliverance, like Jesus or the disciples did. Yet, he commanded the disciples to teach us to obey everything he commanded them—which includes the command to cast out demons and heal the sick (Mt 28:16f). This gap between what the Bible taught and what we experienced always troubled me. I had an encounter with Jesus when I was nineteen and surrendered my life to him. That encountered ignited my weak faith with passion. The passion of my heart was for revival—for the Church to be filled with the Spirit and once again demonstrate the power of Christ to this generation so we could see a great harvest.

When I was twenty-five years old, a woman came into my office who had come out of witchcraft; she was tormented, and I had to lead her through deliverance. I had never done it, but Jesus got her free. Since then, I have seen thousands of people freed and healed.

Sometimes pastors read the Gospels and preach, "This is who Jesus *was*, and this is what Jesus *did*." But Jesus hasn't changed. The truth is: "This is who Jesus *is*, and this is what Jesus *does*." Jesus came to cast out demons, heal the sick, save the lost, and set the captives free. That's the work of the church!

This is why Doug has written an important book. He wants to help restore deliverance and healing to the church. So do I and so does Jesus. I'll tell you two reasons why I believe this is so critical, to Light up the Dark. First, we need to restore deliverance and healing ministries to the church because there are many in the church who are bound by Satan and will never be as effective as they can be without first being freed. Having led hundreds of Soul Care Conferences and equipped many people to walk with the Spirit and do the works of the kingdom, I have seen and heard thousands of testimonies of once bound Christians who have encountered the liberating power of Jesus Christ and were never the same again. I have seen countless numbers of believers who were stuck and unfruitful in their Christian lives, until after they experienced deliverance. I do not believe we will see revival until this ministry of Jesus is restored to the church. Jesus wasn't a country bumpkin who couldn't discern between a psychological problem and a demonic issue. He did deliverance because it was absolutely necessary. We must return to it.

Second, we need to restore deliverance and healing to the church for the sake of reaching people for Christ. In a pluralistic, syncretistic society where all deities are considered equal, only the unequal display of Jesus's power will convince people of the supremacy of Christ. One of the primary reasons why the Gospel advanced so dramatically in the early church was because the ministry of Jesus was being carried on by the followers of Christ and the Kingdom of God was being demonstrated in power. These pagan converts knew the power of demonic deities, but they discovered

Jesus was unequaled in power and compassion. More people are going to come to Christ today because they know they are broken and in need of a healer, than because they know they are sinners in need of a Savior. People are aware of their brokenness, and they need the power of Jesus to be set free.

This is who Jesus *is*, and this is what Jesus *does*. Jesus heals; Jesus delivers. Doug shows that historically and demonstrates convincingly how lives are being changed still today. The book is littered with testimonies of people who have been changed by the ongoing ministry of Jesus. Jesus hasn't changed and neither has his message.

Read the book. Get the help you need to live it out. Pastors and leaders, bring it back into the culture of your church. Do it wisely. Do it carefully. Do it compassionately. Do it without all of the excesses. But do it. This is the message of Jesus. This is kingdom normal!

—Dr. Rob Reimer
author of *Soul Care*
www.renewalinternational.org

ACKNOWLEDGEMENTS

My life is the sum of a great many parts; that is, a great number of people who have built into my experience. Relative to the content of this book, there are many who helped shape my view and familiarity with aspects of the supernatural. Their contributions are expressed in the pages that follow. I am grateful for Pastor Len Z., who prayed for me for the filling of the Holy Spirit when I was fifteen years of age. I am grateful for Jim and Brenda Regehr who first introduced me to concepts of spiritual warfare when I was a young pastor. I am grateful for mentors who led me towards my personal journey of healing and deliverance, Dr. Ken Driedger, Melanie Driedger, Dr. Martin Sanders, Dr. Ingrid Davis, Maureen Guardacosta, and Dr. Rob Reimer. I am grateful for peers who have spurred me on in this regard and towards the project that is now this book; Dr. Ron Brown, Dr. Sandy Isfeld, Johnny Thiessen, Scott Dixon, and Graham English. I am grateful for the team in which I serve at the Western Canadian District of the Christian and Missionary Alliance and its Superintendent, Brent Trask, for supporting and encouraging my doctoral studies which form the basis of this book.

Numerous people generously shared their personal stories of healing and deliverance that are found in these pages; Dr. Lisa

Burchett, Michel Dube', Ken Fisher, Jake (Jacquie) Fraser, Maureen Guardacosta, Kyle Harnett, Heather Heywood, Laurie McLean, Erin Reed, Brent Rushinka, Scott Whitford, and Jordy van Dyck.

Still others poured over the earlier drafts, providing critical feedback and substantive suggestions for improvement, Teri Balzer, Dr. Ron Brown, Michelle Derksen, Doug Doyle, Dr. Roger Helland, Dr. Mabiala Justin-Robert Kenzo, Elizabeth Lim, Brent Rushinka, and Dr. Rob Snow. Many thanks to you all for your helpful contributions!

INTRODUCTION

HOW TO READ THIS BOOK

Arise, shine, for your light has come,
and the glory of the Lord rises upon you.
See, darkness covers the earth
and thick darkness is over the peoples,
but the Lord rises upon you
and his glory appears over you.
Nations will come to your light,
and kings to the brightness of your dawn.

—Isaiah 60:1-3

I used to live in the city of Fort McMurray, in Northern Alberta. In many ways, it's a city of extremes. Being the "face" to Canada's oil industry and possessing the third largest oil reserve in the world, Fort McMurray predictably experiences the extremes of cyclical commodity booms and busts. Because of its northern location, Fort McMurray experiences extreme ranges in temperature, all the way from minus 40° Celsius in winter to plus 35° in summer.

On June 21, the summer solstice, it doesn't get completely dark during the night. This is the longest day of the year for the northern hemisphere, with the sun rising and setting at 3:34 a.m. and 9:23 p.m. With there being close to eighteen hours of sunlight, seventy-four percent of the day has daylight. This had a direct effect on my energy level. I needed less sleep. It wouldn't be uncommon to see people going for walks or doing errands in their yards at midnight when it would still seem like dusk. In contrast, during the winter solstice, the sun rises at 9:00 a.m. and sets at 3:47 p.m., not even seven hours of sunlight, representing merely twenty-eight percent of the day.

My office didn't have a window, and I would frequently go days without meaningful exposure to natural light. I struggled to live with such limited exposure to sunlight. This also had a direct effect on my energy level. Now I needed more sleep. This affected the way people lived—it wouldn't be uncommon for people to go extended periods without emerging from their homes. Light is life-giving. Darkness is energy-robbing.

Today I begin to write this book during the Winter Solstice; December 21, the longest night of the year. This is also the season of Advent, the season of lights in the midst of darkness. A classic Advent scripture is found in Isaiah 9:2, *"The people walking in darkness have seen a great light; on those living in the land of deep darkness a light has dawned."*

This text was of deep inspiration to George Frideric Handel who composed an oratorio in 1741, what has become commonly known as *Handel's Messiah*. This text was also inspirational to C.S. Lewis as he wrote a metaphor of the cosmic struggle between darkness and light in his Narnia series. This is the gospel, the gospel of light. The light seen by people in darkness is the Emmanuel, God (now) with us. This is the reason why the Christmas season is so deeply characterized by lights, candles, and decorations. Darkness hasn't won. Light has won. Jesus has and is lighting up the dark.

I am writing this book to help the church rediscover the enduring and brilliant light of the Gospel of Jesus Christ in all its fullness. Yes, the gospel is a cognitive message but so very much more! It is light that changes the nature of every part of our lives, our communities, and our world. A facet of this gospel is the work of Jesus represented in healing and deliverance, two words that have regrettably caused much confusion, fear, and dissonance in the church. Too many Christ-followers find themselves in one of two ditches when it comes to their understanding and practice of healing and deliverance.

One ditch is characterized by fear. Some may be fearful of extremes they have seen expressed in these ministries. Images may come to mind of people screaming, grotesque bodily wretching, self-serving televangelists, suspect claims of the miraculous, and all-too-often associated with an appeal for people to open their wallets. I don't fear such experiences as much as I grieve them. I also distance myself from such harmful and corrupted representations of Jesus in healing and deliverance.

Some may have hesitation to pursue healing because of fear or disappointment around the question, "What if God doesn't heal?" Past prayerful attempts may have come up short. Perhaps God didn't "show up," and they now find themselves wounded, calloused, or skeptical. All of which is understandable. I, too, have walked that journey, including the loss of a child through illness.

This ditch may also be characterized by unfamiliarity, the mere lack of experiential knowledge on the subject. Many people in the church have received little or no teaching. Here, people may be trapped in an Enlightenment view of the world, where the *only* perspective to have is through the lens of empirical, scientific evidence. This myopic perspective has significantly affected both the theology and more so the practice of the church in the West. The distance between that which we read in the scriptures and what we observe in the church is far too wide. I deeply grieve the perspectives and practices (or lack thereof) of this ditch.

The second ditch is characterized by the idolatrous exploit of the ministries of healing and deliverance for selfish gain. Rather than a response to humbly follow Jesus and allow him to set the agenda, these ditch-dwellers attempt to build a ministry upon self-aggrandizement and sensationalism. One tell-tale of such peril is a ministry that sees the "supernatural" limited to the public stage and through their proclaimed spiritual elites. Rather, Jesus intended all of his followers to function as his body, with no singular individuals subtly attempting to capture the glory and credit.

It is my hope and prayer that *Light Up the Dark* might help Jesus-followers and the broader church avoid such ditches and travel more in the center of the road, seeing their ministries built upon the ministry and example of Jesus Christ. I will attempt to do so by providing biblical, historical, and evidential foundations to the ministries of healing and deliverance, thereby demonstrating how they are critical (though not exclusive) facets of the disciple-making process. A good measure of the content of these pages finds their roots in my doctoral dissertation, *The Effect of Deliverance on the Well-being of Christian Leaders* (2019), as well as related courses I have taught at Ambrose University and Seminary. As such, the weighting of material will admittedly be towards deliverance over physical healing. This, however, is not regrettable on my part as I perceive the church to have less confusion and more acceptance of the ministry of healing than deliverance, although as I will demonstrate, they are frequently deeply related.

HOW TO READ THIS BOOK

Light Up the Dark has been written to be consumed in two ways: as one coherent read, and also as a more accessible reference tool. It has been written in three parts, each with shorter chapters that might be better accessed by church leaders developing their own teaching frameworks. Much of the material comes from a body of literature on these topics that, although valuable, are highly academic and not so easily accessible to the non-academic reader. This book is an attempt to provide something of a general overview, hoping to reasonably represent the greater consensus of the broader literature. Wherever pertinent I have included citations of other sources to aid students of this subject in their own research pursuits.

Part 1, *The Problem of Worldview*, deals with cultural perspectives pertaining to healing and deliverance. The scriptures seem to present a view of reality that significantly differs from the church in the West. I will illustrate how we arrived at such a place and present an alternative for the church to consider; one that embraces both the natural and supernatural, the Gospel of the Kingdom of Light, and the vehicle of multiplying disciples as Jesus's intended means for his mission. These chapters provide a framework for understanding and appreciating the sections that follow, especially for those that have limited background and understanding in healing and deliverance.

Part 2 will dive into *The Evidence of History*, from the Old Testament, the Gospels, the Apostles, the Early Church Fathers, the Dark Ages, and Reformers. I will attempt to answer the question: "If Jesus and his disciples performed miracles as a norm of their ministry, and the church so rarely does today... what happened?" I will also discuss the more recent rise of healing and deliverance ministries and their various streams of influence.

Part 3 will explore *The Research and Onramps*. The research is a summation of the data collected and interpreted specific to my doctoral research project, which to my knowledge is the first-ever study of this kind. These chapters will highlight many enlightening discoveries that invite Christ-followers to allow God to redefine their view of normal, one that is significantly characterized by the defeat of darkness and the increased presence of light. A series of onramps are given as recommendations to the church, providing pathways for her to forge a way into an experience that better reflects the posture and practices of Christ himself.

This book is more about the who, what, when, where, and why, of healing and deliverance, than it is about the how. I do, however, provide numerous onramps to help the curious move forward with thoughtful intent. Additionally, I make numerous recommendations of excellent resources that will be helpful in equipping people to function fruitfully and "in the center of the road" as they pursue ministries of healing and deliverance.

The chapters before us are illustrated with narratives of people both receiving and releasing healing and deliverance. Many of these will be somewhat helpful to better understand how these ministries might function. These are short narratives of individuals who have deeply experienced Jesus *lighting up their darkness*. Some of these people were represented in my dissertation project—quantifying the effect of deliverance upon the well-being of Christian leaders. These vignettes serve to illustrate the backdrop of material that is largely theological, historical, and evidential.

My friend Graham English shared a picture with me that represents my hope for the church in this regard: the tamarisk tree. In Genesis 21:33, *"Abraham planted a tamarisk tree in Beersheba, and there he called upon the name of the Lord, the Eternal God."* The tamarisk can be found in numerous settings, even in the desert where it has proven to be hardy against drought and heat. It survives these harsh conditions by growing a deep taproot, accessing nutrients far beneath it. As such, it grows very slowly in the desert.

Abraham planted the tamarisk not for himself to enjoy but for future generations. I write, not so much with great hopes that the current church will make the needed seismic shifts in the coming year or two. Rather, that the emerging leaders of today and the yet-to-be-discovered leaders of tomorrow will see the gospel as more brilliant and more deeply transformational than previous generations. It took the church 1,700 years to fall into our current hole of neglect and ignorance; it will take a little while to climb back out, even with God's richest grace. I dream of a day when children growing up in the Kingdom of God can't perceive a church that doesn't make disciples that make disciples, frequently characterized by personal experiences of freedom through healing and deliverance. I'm in it for the long game.

Additionally, the tamarisk tree multiplies through the flowers it produces. Each flower generates thousands of tiny, one-millimeter seeds that can be easily carried in the wind to distant places. I pray that the Prince of Peace, the Light of the World, would be welcomed in your heart, to bring the hope of light to dim and dark places, to invite you into a deeper experience of the Gospel of Light. I pray that these seeds of light would find their ways to every tribe, tongue, and nation to bear uniquely and refractorily the brilliance of Jesus Christ.

PART ONE

THE PROBLEM OF WORLDVIEW

CHAPTER ONE

THE REALITY GAP

Now the earth was formless and empty, darkness was over the surface of the deep and the Spirit of God was hovering over the waters. And God said, 'Let there be light,' and there was light.
                                        —Genesis 1:2-3

I had heard about the ancient city of Petra. I had heard about it, but I had not yet visited. Because I had not seen Petra, there was a gap of reality between what I perceived and what is. I had seen incredible pictures of this city, built two thousand five hundred years ago by the now-extinct Nabataean kingdom. From a distance, I admired this long-lost community that once held twenty-thousand residents with many of the "buildings" chiseled out of the rose-colored rock faces of the canyon it occupies. I had seen the famous Treasury of Petra in the film *Indiana Jones and the Last Crusade*. I recognized it as one of the ancient wonders of the world.

In 2006 I was able to go to Jordan and visit Petra. On my one-day visit, I resolved to take only a few pictures. I wanted to experience Petra not through the lens of a camera but through the lens of my own eyes. I walked down the *Siq*, the 1.2-kilometer descending gorge that functions as the gateway to the city. The winding pathway was something of a tease, with each bend holding promise of the famed Treasury to come into view. Anticipation grew as I didn't know how close or how far I was. And then, finally, Petra came into view, and I stood in front of the Treasury and beheld its historic splendor. Petra, it turned out, was way better than I knew. Only through personal experience could I bridge my reality gap and come to appreciate her more deeply.

Jesus and his gospel are way better than we know. Because God is intrinsically an infinite being, we can't come to a complete understanding of him, there is always more to discover. His gospel, his good news, is better news than any of us have fully realized or experienced. The transformational work of Jesus must yet be more fully realized in our lives. Such was the case for many, many people who came into contact with Jesus when he walked the Earth. In him, they found acceptance, joy, healing, and freedom from evil spirits; and I'm not speaking metaphorically. Jesus (and his work in people's lives) is as real as it gets.

OVERCOMING A NARROW WORLD VIEW

Perhaps one of the most significant challenges of the modern church is overcoming a myopic worldview, a perspective of reality that limits the perception of Jesus's brilliance. Our personal collections of pain, disappointment, distractions, and disillusionments risk diminishing our understanding and experience of who Jesus is, why he came, and of his capabilities today. Our current understanding of his gospel tends to form limitations or riverbanks in our minds of what he will do. We tend to get boxed in and have a view of God that is limited rather than limitless. God, by his very nature, is limitless.

All of this naturally forms a *reality gap,* and none of us can entirely escape it; it is a fact of life. A gap between what Jesus's true intentions and capabilities are and our acceptance of what is normal. A gap between our perception of reality and the eternal reality—the reality that Jesus sees through his eyes. Most of us are subject to our own confirmation biases. What we perceive to be our reality, over time, becomes our understanding of reality. If we haven't witnessed healings or deliverances from evil spirits, we tend to believe these things don't exist or, at the very least, that they are not regular occurrences. Oh, to see things as he sees them. Oh, to see ourselves as he sees us.

A way to define spiritual maturity might be the journey towards narrowing the gap between our perceived reality and God, the ultimate truth. To travel the pages in this book is to pursue a narrowing of this gap. Specifically, this journey will establish more solid foundations from scripture, history, and research on healing and deliverance from evil spirits.

MACRO-LENSES TO VIEW THE WORLD

The lens through which one views the ancient Christian scriptures will significantly determine their interpretation of them, including matters of supernatural activity. There are several "macro-themes" in the scriptures through which we can view the entirety of written scripture. For instance, there is the theme of freedom versus bondage and slavery. God created the world with untold freedom until humanity chose a destiny apart from God's provision, which led to their bondage. Christ came to free humanity from the bondage of the kingdom of darkness and restore freedom. He came to pick a fight with the slave driver. As C.S. Lewis once wrote, "The incarnation is an act of war."

Another macro-narrative is that of the garden versus exile. Humanity was created to walk closely in relationship with its creator, represented by the garden. As humanity chose to fulfill their destiny apart from God, they found themselves exiled from his presence. Christ came to return humanity from exile to the garden, the place of God's presence.

Yet another macro-narrative is that of light versus darkness, and this is by no means a minor macro lens through which to view all of scripture and perceive ultimate reality. God's first creative act was to light up the dark.

> *Now the earth was formless and empty, darkness was over the surface of the deep, and the Spirit of God was hovering over the waters. And God said, "Let there be light," and there was light.*
> —Genesis 1:2-3

Light illuminates everything we know. Light defined everything that followed God's initial creative acts. Then humanity chose darkness. Christ came into the world to restore light. People who experience darkness can now see a great light; Jesus, the light of the world (John 9:5). This is the hope of Advent, the realization of Christmas, and the victory of Easter. Countless books and movies have been written using the motif of light versus darkness. From *Star Wars* to *Narnia* and from Shakespeare to Dickens, the world of art and literature gives testament to this battle in all facets of culture throughout humanity's long history.

THE SUPREMACY OF LIGHT

Light conquers darkness. Always. Darkness has no power over light. Absolute darkness has zero power over a small candle in a room. There is no viable contest. Light wins every time. The invitation to welcome God's glorious light is intensely personal. Wherever there are shadows or darkness, the hope of light compels us towards a different, redeeming reality. This is, in effect, the gospel. This is also a word to those who approach the demonic realm with trepidation; light has absolute power over darkness. Fear isn't needed nor recommended when dealing with darkness. Light is a really big deal, and Jesus has no end of it.

The other bookend of scripture presents a case for light as well. In the culmination of all things, we see that ultimately, in Christ, God has lit up the dark.

No longer will there be any curse. The throne of God and of the Lamb will be in the city, and his servants will serve him. They will see his face, and his name will be on their foreheads. There will be no more night. They will not need the light of a lamp or the light of the sun, for the Lord God will give them light. And they will reign for ever and ever.

—Revelation 22:3-5

We know the beginning; there was light. We know the ending; there is light. We live somewhere in the middle; we are emerging out of the shadows of darkness into God's glorious light. This is why Jesus came. He came for us, and his light is far greater than we know.

HEALING AND DELIVERANCE: FACETS OF LIGHT

The prophets forecast the ministry of Jesus as being characterized by light defeating darkness.

The people walking in darkness have seen a great light; on those living in the land of deep darkness a light has dawned.

—Isaiah 9:2

As presented in the Gospels, Jesus's ministry is most consistently described as the proclamation of good news, healing the sick, and setting captives free. Jesus came to free people captive to demons. This light emerged against a backdrop of overwhelming darkness. Yet the modern church in the West has frequently reduced Jesus's view of salvation to an uttered prayer to 'get you to heaven.'

Jesus saw his ministry of light as deeply holistic. He illuminated eternal trajectories but also people's physical, material, emotional, and relational being, emanating into every facet of society with hope and wellness. Perhaps the best word to describe his holistic approach is a word written in the original Greek texts of the Gospels, *sozo*. *Sozo* is one of those words that doesn't easily translate into English. It is used fifty-four times in the four Gospels of Matthew, Mark, Luke, and John and over one hundred times in the New Testament. It can mean several things, and Jesus used it frequently.

For example, *sozo* is used to describe Jesus's work of saving people, forgiving their sin, and providing salvation from the curse of sin. It is used in this way thirty-eight times.

She will bear a son, and you shall call his name Jesus, for he will save [sozo] his people from their sins.
—Matthew 1:21

Those along the path are the ones who hear, and then the devil comes and takes away the word from their hearts, so that they may not believe and be saved [sozo].
—Luke 8:12

To be clear, Jesus does care about our eternal trajectory, the locale of our eternal being, whether that be in the presence of God (eternal light) or away from God's presence (eternal darkness). He has provided a way for all to escape the eternal curse of sin and death.

Sozo is also used to describe physical healing or resurrection at least twenty times in the Gospels. On one occasion, the daughter of a synagogue ruler, Jarius, had died. Before Jesus raised her from the dead, he said, *"Don't be afraid; just believe, and she will be healed [sozo]"* (Luke 8:50).

Another time, a woman who had suffered hemorrhaging for twelve years reached out to touch his cloak, believing in faith that Jesus had the power to heal. Jesus responded, *"... Take heart, daughter,' he said, 'your faith has healed [sozo] you'"* (Matthew 9:22).

Some translations render the word *sozo* in these and other accounts as "made well," or "made whole." Other usages of *sozo* in the New Testament refer to demonic deliverance. Jesus once encountered a significantly demonized man whose life was all but destroyed. After Jesus cast out the demons, Luke describes the following, *"Those who had seen it told the people how the demon-possessed man had been cured [sozo]"* (Luke 8:36).

The single word, *sozo,* means many things: healing, deliverance, salvation, wholeness, rescue, restoration, and a cure. It is less about merely calling out darkness and so much more about restoring light. As the light of the world, Jesus set in motion his cosmic plan of restoring all things, curing all things, and rescuing all things to himself. In lighting up the dark, he set out to bring his version of reality to earth, one that is better and brighter than the one we are experiencing. His methodology was not via political activism or violent cultural revolution but rather through people receiving his sozo ministry, each person allowing Christ to shine his light into their darkness.

My aim in this book is to help us better understand sozo, God's holistic intent. This includes his work of divine healing and deliverance from the power of spirits of darkness. To be clear, I am not characterizing healing and deliverance as the full extent of God's sozo work. Even so, one can't fully perceive his redemptive work without the ministry of healing and deliverance in the lives of individuals.

AN INVITATION TO HOPE

One might assume this book is about demons and illness. It is much more about healing and freedom. Demonic forces and illnesses are elements that Jesus came to bring ultimate freedom from. On this side of the grave, we can taste deeply what will be perfected in eternity. For some, this book might provide an onramp to hope. Perhaps they have never welcomed the light of Jesus into their life through a personal relationship with him. Jesus invites us into that!

For others who have known Jesus, this book might serve as an onramp to a deeper and richer experience of Christ's transforming presence. We can embrace the hope that the yet-to-be-redeemed darkness in our lives could be diminished or eliminated. Hope that something of God's divine presence might touch our body, emotions, memories, and relationships. Again, Jesus is way better than we know.

Still, for others, perhaps this book will grant them the confidence to champion disciple-making with healing and deliverance as critical facets. Perhaps a stronger biblical, historical, and evidential foundation will give them the requisite boldness to lead their life, ministry, and church into more careful alignment with Christ's enduring ministries of freedom and *sozo*.

KERRY'S FREEDOM FROM ANGER

Kerry had attended our church for many years. He and his wife were diligent attendees who seemed content. At age sixty-two, Kerry reached out to one of my deliverance team members and me. He expressed that he had anger issues, with episodes that were only getting worse, sometimes erupting daily. He had "always" been angry and wanted to no longer take it out on his family.

Kerry had come to a place where he was willing to try anything to experience some relief. When we met with Kerry, we prayed for Holy Spirit to fill the room and to guide us as we sought Christ's freedom for him. We declared in Jesus's name that anything evil that would seek to block what God had for Kerry would leave in the name of Jesus, not being allowed to interfere. At this moment (which is expected in my spiritual gifting of discernment of spirits), the demon attached to Kerry became visible to me, and he roared over Kerry in an expression of rage.

After hearing parts of his story, I asked Kerry very simply if there was a moment in his life that stuck out to him as the beginning of his anger. He informed us that when he was twelve, an adult family friend had come to visit Kerry's family. This man had visited several times and had often molested Kerry during those visits. Upon this latest visit, Kerry loaded a shotgun, pointed it at that man, and screamed he would kill him for what he had done. Kerry told us that he remembered being so filled with rage that he couldn't control what he was doing. He recalled that something invisible had come and lowered the shotgun, so it was no longer pointed at his abuser. Kerry insisted that he had known his whole life that it was an angel who had lowered the gun because he had every intent to kill his abuser. The abuser ran from the house, never to return. From then on, Kerry had struggled with uncontrollable rage.

I then led Kerry in a forgiveness prayer for his abuser and prayers that broke all soul ties with his abuser. We took authority over the demon attached to Kerry, making it truthfully answer whether it had any more rights to stay in Kerry's life. Its answer was "no." We both then listened to the Holy Spirit for any other roots of anger in Kerry's life. When we both felt peace with Holy Spirit that there were no more roots, I had Kerry repeat after me: "In Jesus name, I bind and gag all spirits of rage and anger that attached to me through the abuse of _____(abuser's name), and I send it all to where Jesus sends it, taking its work with it." The demon was cast out, and Kerry began to cry. He looked up at us and asked, "Is this what true peace feels like?"

Within one week, Kerry's mother approached me at church and said, "My son is a different man." Kerry continued on a journey of freedom and joy. Approximately two years later, as Kerry lay in a hospital with terminal pancreatic cancer, he took one of my hands and said, "Please don't ever stop what you are doing in bringing Jesus's freedom to people. I am so grateful that these last two years have been filled with joy and peace. Now I look forward to seeing my Savior." To this day, when discouragement comes, I think of Kerry, and he is often my inspiration for pressing forward into the ministry God has called me.

A NEEDED WORLDVIEW SHIFT

The church in the West needs a worldview shift. The church has been conditioned to view a gospel that is too narrow and the power of God as inaccessible (I will demonstrate this in chapters that follow). Yet Jesus has commissioned his church to light up the dark. Jesus commissioned the Apostle Paul with these words,

> *... I have appeared to you to appoint you as a servant and as a witness of what you have seen and will see of me. I will rescue you from your own people and from the Gentiles. I am sending you to them to open their eyes and turn them from darkness to light, and from the power of Satan to God, so that they may receive forgiveness of sins and a place among those who are sanctified by faith in me.'*

—Acts 26:16-18

Jesus invites us as his church to participate in his work of *sozo*, of lighting up the dark. His desired work in our lives and through our lives is more holistic than one can imagine. Any place his light travels dispels darkness. To participate in the advance of his light and to equip others to do the same is what it means to make disciples. This is Jesus's primary mandate to his church; to make disciples who can make disciples.

Jesus never sent anyone on mission without first training and equipping them to proclaim the gospel, heal the sick, and cast out demons. He prepared the twelve disciples in this before sending them out in Luke 9. He did the same thing again in sending out the seventy-two in Luke 10. These chapters establish the ministries of healing and deliverance as critical facets of disciple-making. They don't equate to the total of what it means to make disciples that make disciples. There are other critical elements, such as the place of scripture, prayer, community, service, and so forth. However, to neglect healing and deliverance in the equipping of the church is to significantly miss why Jesus came. Such an omission substantially neglects how much freedom Jesus came to bring, to light up the dark, and it impairs the church's mandate in introducing the gospel—the good news—to the nations.

See, darkness covers the earth
And thick darkness is over the peoples,
But the Lord rises upon you.
Nations will come to your light,
And kings to the brightness of your dawn.

—Isaiah 60:2

CHAPTER TWO

THE CLASH OF KINGDOMS

There are a thousand hacking at the branches of evil
to one who is striking at the root.

—Henry David Thoreau

I f ever passing through Oxford, be sure to stop by *The Eagle and Child* pub. This seventeenth-century pub is surrounded by the highest places of learning over the last millennia; universities dating back to 1096. Aside from its history and the premium pints served daily, one will find something else most interesting at *The Eagle and Child*. Walk to the rear of the pub and enter The Rabbit Room, adorned by a simple wooden table next to a glowing stone fireplace. Above the mantel and next to a portrait of C. S. Lewis, note the sign hung on the wall,

> C.S. Lewis, his brother, W.H. Lewis, J.R.R. Tolkien, Charles Williams and other friends met every Tuesday morning, between the years 1939–1962 in the back room of this their favourite pub. These men, popularly known as the "Inklings," met here to drink Beer and to discuss, among other things, the books they were writing.

Several things capture my attention here, the least of which is not that beer is capitalized and consumed in the *morning*. I think I would have liked these guys. But the more incredible wonder is that this table hosted weekly some of the greatest literary minds of the twentieth century, namely C.S. Lewis, of Narnia lore, and J.R.R. Tolkien, the pen behind *The Lord of the Rings* trilogy. Oh, to have been a fly on the wall, listening in on these conversations that spanned decades and would doubtlessly have covered broad subjects such as art, sports, politics, economics, faith, and literature. It was the fusion of these latter two that gave birth to the famous narratives that Lewis and Tolkien created.

Both the *Narnia* and *The Lord of the Rings* series share something in common; they tell the story of the clash of kingdoms. Good versus evil. Freedom versus oppression. Light versus darkness. Kingdoms of freedom versus kingdoms of bondage. No doubt Lewis and Tolkien indelibly influenced each other as their specific writings are metaphors of the same reality: a battle between the Kingdom of Light and the kingdom of darkness. And light ultimately wins.

The tale of these two kingdoms serves as a bookend to all of scripture, from Genesis to the end of Revelation. To understand the Kingdom of God is to understand that light defeats darkness, including the healing of illnesses, and deliverance from evil spirits. To understand healing and deliverance is to understand the Kingdom of God. However, things didn't start with the Kingdom of God on earth, but rather the rule (kingdom) of humanity.

ORIGINS OF THE KINGDOMS OF LIGHT AND DARKNESS

In Genesis 1:28, after creating Adam and Eve, God commissioned them to rule over his creation. In effect, he placed them in a position of authority, in their own kingdom, as it were. They did nothing to deserve this. They did nothing to earn this. God simply loved people. God intended to walk in close relationship with humanity, the centerpiece of his creative work. He intended that people would exercise rulership and stewardship over his creation while *at the same time* enjoying a close relationship with their creator. In God's words, such a scenario was "very good." God's original (and enduring) mission was to partner with humanity to oversee the prosperity of planet earth.

Even in this *very good* situation, God knew that authentic love required choice. God chose to love people. People needed to have the option to love God or not; otherwise, they would exist under tyranny rather than freedom. He framed this choice by forbidding them yet giving them freedom to eat of the Tree of the Knowledge of Good and Evil. Sometime later, things fell apart. Perhaps these first humans were bored, or prideful, or both. Regardless, they fell prey to a bad actor in the narrative, the serpent.

Don't miss that the serpent in the Garden of Eden in Genesis 3 had no intrinsic power or authority over humanity. He didn't rule over the earth. He was merely present, and the only power he had was the power of suggestion.

> *"Did God really say, 'You must not eat from any tree in the garden'?"*
>
> —Genesis 3:1

The bait was hooked, and humanity began to travel down a path of rulership without a relationship with their Creator. This formed the basis of the curse, the kingdom of darkness. Genesis 3 demonstrates that this curse, which humanity allowed on itself, was characterized by pain, difficulty, misogyny, and death (illness), among many, many other negative traits. What was very good had now become cursed. Freedom was replaced with tyranny. The light of freedom dimmed. This is the origin of the reign of the kingdom of darkness on earth. Healing and deliverance from the kingdom of darkness was needed for all that was broken.

REALITIES OF DEMONIC PRESENCE

Belief in demonic realities and demonic possession is reflected in seventy-four percent of societies in today's world.[1] It isn't hard to see the effects of the existence of dark spirits today. Despite substantive progress gifted to us by scientific advances of The Enlightenment, slavery has never been more prevalent, predominantly via the sex trade. Human trafficking is on the rise. Forced organ harvesting occurs regularly in some parts of the world. Attempts of genocide marked the twentieth century numerous times. The list can go on and on; clearly, the curse is still with us.

Jesus concurred. During his forty days in the wilderness, he was tempted by the devil, and the conversation involved who was presiding over the world.

> *The devil led him up to a high place and showed him in an instant all the kingdoms of the world. And he said to him, "I will give you all their authority and splendor; it has been given to me, and I can give it to anyone I want to. If you worship me, it will all be yours."*
>
> —Luke 4:5-7

Interestingly, Jesus didn't refute the devil's claim that the kingdoms of the world had been given to him. They had been.

---

[1] Craig S. Keener, *Miracles: The Credibility of the New Testament Accounts* (Grand Rapids, MI: Baker Academic Press, 2011), vol. 2, 791, quoting Erika Bourguignon in *Spirit Possession Belief* (1976) states, "...belief in spirit possession is widespread in varied cultures around the world, 'as any reader of ethnographies knows.' She sampled 488 diverse, ethnographically representative societies and discovered spirit possession beliefs in 360 societies, that is, 74 percent of those studies."

Not by God, but by rebellious and prideful humanity, thinking they would be better off without God. The result was that all of creation, including humanity, were now living under the kingdom of darkness.

GOD IS NOT IN CONTROL, YET SOVEREIGN

I frequently hear Christians stating that "God is in control" as they observe a broken and disturbed world. I disagree with them. God is in control of the Kingdom of God. He is in control of those who have surrendered their lives to him. But he isn't in control of all the events on earth. God is sovereign, but he is not in "control." He doesn't control the sex trade industry. He doesn't control the car careening off the road to kill the father of young children. He doesn't control the structures that abuse people, support poverty, and destroy the planet's environment. He gave these things over to humanity to oversee, that is, to control. We, in turn, surrendered this authority to the kingdom of darkness.

The Apostle John describes the dire cosmic situation this way, *"We know that we are children of God, and that the whole world is under the control of the evil one"* (1 John 5:19).

To believe that God is in control means being naïve regarding the kingdom of darkness. This naivety leads many people to unnecessary pain and confusion. "Why did God allow this to happen?" "Why does God allow suffering in the world?" These are the wrong questions.

God isn't in control of these things, and yet he is sovereign. His purposes will ultimately reign. We know the final chapter, and it reveals that Jesus is the victor over all things. The Kingdom of Light triumphs over the kingdom of darkness. This is what it means to pray, "Your kingdom come, your will be done," to

participate in the advance of the Kingdom of Light over the kingdom of darkness.

HEALING FROM A FATHER'S SUICIDE

*I (Scott) was carrying the weight of a broken identity and didn't know it.
Over time, the suicide of my biological father at the age of five simply became
a sad part of my story. I remember grieving, I remember the funeral, and I
remember fragments of the time following. The tragedy had a definite impact
on my developmental years, but I don't remember experiencing any other
weight than the weight of grief and the permanence of the loss.*

*Thirty-five years later, while at a conference with a group of fellow
pastors, I found freedom from a pain I had never identified. During a time
of prayer, one of my colleagues (who had been operating for some time in the
areas of deliverance, healing, inner healing, etc.) sensed that Holy Spirit
wanted to explore this issue with me. I had shared earlier with them the story
of my father's passing. As he prayed for me, he asked me to allow Jesus to put
a picture in my mind of the time frame of my father's passing.*

*Immediately, I was five years old in my memory… walking up the stairs
of the hotel/bar my parents owned at the time. There was no one else around
in this "motion-picture" moment. Somehow, I knew that I needed to enter
the room at the top of the stairs, knowing that this was the room where the
event occurred—even though I didn't previously know where it took place.
My colleague continued to pray and guide this inner-healing experience, asking Jesus to reveal himself in this memory/moment and asking me to report to
him what I was seeing and experiencing as the scene unfolded.*

*I glanced into the room, now feeling something deep within me begin
to come closer to the surface of my soul, but without any sense of fear. Jesus
was standing in the center of the room, standing over my deceased father.
As I stood there in the doorway, he looked at me over his left shoulder. My
colleague asked if Jesus was saying anything or if I was saying anything to*

him. Jesus was silent, but a question flowed from deep in my soul that seems obvious but had a much deeper personal meaning. In my mind's eye, I asked Jesus, "Why did this happen?" The question had nothing to do with circumstance; it had to do with my five-year-old self, wondering if he was too much "boy" for his father to handle—wondering if, in a way, that he (I) was partly responsible for his father taking his own life.

Very quietly, with a tear running down his left cheek as he was looking at me, Jesus said: "This happened because your father was hurting and there was no one to help him." The dam burst! A torrent of deeply rooted and hard-packed emotion flooded out of me in a moment of release, relief, and healing. I received the answer to a question I had never directly asked or identified in these words from Jesus. In these words, I found peace, and part of my identity was healed. These words also became a commissioning for me to help as many people as possible to discover this same freedom. Through training and Holy Spirit empowerment, it has been an honor to help dozens upon dozens of people find similar freedom. My identity continues to grow, and my leadership has flourished since this moment. I am deeply grateful to my colleague and friend, and Jesus for this life-changing encounter!

EMERGENCE OF THE KINGDOM OF LIGHT

Very early in the scriptures, God saw the clash of the kingdoms emerging. The first prophetic reference to the need for a messiah figure is found in Genesis 3:15. In speaking to the serpent, God says, "… I will put enmity between you and the woman, and between your offspring and hers; he will crush your head, and you will strike his heel."

This forms the beginning of the anticipated arrival of the Messiah, the Christ and his Kingdom of Light, where the enemy and his curse are defeated. The early Christians understood these connections:

*The God of peace will soon crush Satan
under your feet.*

—Romans 16:20

The reason the Son of God appeared was to destroy the devil's work.
—1 John 3:8

They recognized that a battle raged between the kingdom of darkness and the Kingdom of Light. They realized that humanity was powerless against the kingdom of darkness, for they had already given up their authority. They needed something from outside the kingdom of darkness, *someone* who stood beyond the curse of the kingdom of darkness. They possessed no light in and of themselves. They needed an external source. They understood this is why Jesus came as both fully God and completely human to represent humanity. Only he had extrinsic authority that could trump the kingdom of darkness. They understood that Jesus came to light up the dark.

The god of this age has blinded the minds of unbelievers, so that they cannot see the light of the gospel that displays the glory of Christ, who is the image of God... For God, who said, "Let light shine out of darkness," made his light shine in our hearts to give us the light of the knowledge of God's glory displayed in the face of Christ.

—2 Corinthians 4:4,6

What would this look like to those paying attention? The light would manifest in healing that which was broken and delivering those held captive. The curse would be reversed.

The clash between good and evil in our world is essentially the clash between the kingdom of darkness and the Kingdom of Light.

Images of old spaghetti Western movies come to mind. A dusty old saloon with the tyrannical and illegitimate outlaw gangster sipping his whiskey at the bar. Through the double saloon doors comes the hero who confidently yet quietly states, "There's a new sheriff in town." The narratives of the *Narnia* and *The Lord of the Rings* series communicate well this battle and ultimate defeat of darkness. Tyranny is ending. The curse is being defeated. That which is broken is being healed. Those that are held captive are being released. The new sheriff is lighting up the dark. Surely Lewis and Tolkien discussed these matters. Surely Jesus came for such a purpose.

Rescue from captivity (deliverance) and newfound freedom become predictable hallmarks of the Kingdom of Light as experienced by the church of the first century.

> *...the Father, who has qualified you to share in the inheritance of his holy people in the kingdom of light. For he has rescued us from the dominion of darkness and brought us into the kingdom of the Son he loves, in whom we have redemption, the forgiveness of sins.*
>
> —Colossians 1:12-14

Jesus is the Light of the World. His light shines the brightest in darkness. The words of Jesus to Saul-soon-to-be-Paul on the road to Damascus communicated this Kingdom dynamic:

> *I will rescue you from your own people and from the Gentiles. I am sending you to them to open their eyes and turn them from darkness to light, and from the power of Satan to God, so that they may receive forgiveness of sins and a place among those who are sanctified by faith in me.*
>
> —Acts 26:17,18

The pen of the Apostle Peter also elaborates on the theme of light:

> *But you are a chosen people, a royal priesthood, a holy nation, God's special possession, that you may declare the praises of him who called you out of darkness into his wonderful light.*
>
> —1 Peter 2:9

CHARACTERISTICS OF THE KINGDOM OF LIGHT

The new sheriff, Jesus, arrived in town, and many of those following him thought he was about to lead a political revolution. Some thought that when he spoke of the kingdom of heaven drawing near that he was referring to an earthly dominion. Their hope was the kingdom of Rome being displaced and a redeemed, political kingdom of Israel being restored. Many confused Jesus's intentions in his day. Sadly, many are confused about his work today, erroneously believing his church is about political conquest and a legislated religious society. Still others are deeply confused by thinking the message of Christ is primarily limited to cognitive preaching. While important, gospel proclamation was always intended to be accompanied by experiential transformation. As we will explore later, this partnership was most frequently shown in the Gospels and Acts through experiences of healing and deliverance from demonic spirits.

To know what Jesus's priorities are today, we need to look no further than his priorities during his three-year ministry in first-century Palestine. Jesus's life indeed demonstrated many things: holy living, compassion for the poor, profound teaching, humility, and forgiveness. Yet, the most frequent summary of his ministry includes the following as core elements: he preached the gospel, healed the sick, and cast out demons.[2] The gospel he preached was the gospel of the Kingdom, the newly-arrived Kingdom of Light that was displacing the illegitimate kingdom of darkness.

This wasn't mere cognitive-only good news. This was *experiential* good news. People who were ill and injured received restoration. The Kingdom of God had come near! To others held in crippling captivity from demonic spirits, they received freedom from the tyrant! The Kingdom of Light had come near! This was holistic good news. It was seen, felt, experienced, and heard. This is the gospel—righting the past, healing the present, and securing the future.

---

[2]   I.e., Matthew 4:23,24, 8:14-17, 9:35, 11:4-5, 15:29-31; Mark 1:21-25, 1:27, 1:29-34, 3:7-12, 3:13-15, 6:12-13, 6:53-56; Luke 4:38-44, 6:17-18, 7:21, 9:11.

CHAPTER THREE

THE NATURAL VS. SUPERNATURAL

We see the world, not as it is, but as we are—or, as we are condi-
tioned to see it. When we open our mouths to describe what we see,
we in effect describe ourselves, our perceptions, our paradigms.[3]
—Stephen R. Covey

From both inside and outside the church, many people have an understandable skepticism when it comes to matters such as divine healing and deliverance from demonic spirits. There is certainly no shortage of examples of excesses, abuses, and Christians manipulating such ministries for personal and financial gain. Additionally, in some ways, these things don't mesh well with our modern worldview. There seems to be an ongoing wrestling match between the natural and supernatural worldviews within both the church and broader Western society. This wrestling match leaves many to either under-value or over-value the supernatural activity of God through his church. Conversely, those who traffic in Christian supernatural activity have been dismissive of scientific theory and empirical evidence.

---

3   Stephen R. Covey, *The 7 Habits of Highly Effective People: Restoring the Character Ethic.*
    [Rev. ed.]. (New York: Free Press, 2004).

SCIENCE VS. SUPERNATURAL

Some people may erroneously assume that in order to embrace the ministries of healing and deliverance that one must check their brain at the door and reject a scientific perspective altogether. I see no reason for the realm of the supernatural to compete with science. God created both, and as such, there can be complete congruency. However, we get into trouble when we erroneously refer to the Bible as a science textbook rather than a depiction of God's desire and intention for humanity, ultimately to be in relationship with him through the person of Jesus. Genesis, for example, wasn't written to inform a twenty-first-century scientific mind of the etymology and mechanics of matter. Such a view recklessly forces a scientific worldview upon scripture that didn't exist when such scripture was penned; in other words, it is an interpretive abuse of scripture.

Genesis was written to communicate to the people of its day that: 1) there is only one God, 2) there is no chaotic, competing cosmic battle for supremacy, 3) humanity is the centerpiece of his creative work, ruling and reigning over the Earth, and 4) God desires humanity to exist in a close relationship with himself. To view Genesis as scientifically informative is to violate both the original author and God's purpose for the book.[4]

I love science, which may be surprising to some readers given the subject matter of this book. My personality type thrives on learning and discovery, and some of my favorite conversations are with bona fide scientists: geologists, geneticists, physiologists, and so on. My quality of life has benefited immeasurably because of the scientific method and achievement.

Conversely, we get into trouble when we refer to science as a "meaning-of-life" textbook rather than depicting how things

---

[4]   For more on this subject see *The Lost World of Genesis 1: Ancient Cosmology and the Origins Debate* (2009), by John H. Walton.

around us are and how they came to be. I am comfortable fully embracing science for this latter function, recognizing that even scientific theory ultimately requires, as argued by Aristotle and Thomas Aquinas, an "unmoved mover." A Christian scientific worldview recognizes that any truth discovered through the scientific method is ultimately God's truth as he holds the creative patent! In a sense, science is material theology.

The Age of Enlightenment (approximately 1600–1800 CE) introduced the idea that truth can be objectively measured and observed exclusively from a scientific perspective rather than trusting in the belief of supernatural phenomena. The results of the shift towards a scientific worldview are beyond measure. For example, technological advances in medicine, agriculture, and industry have dramatically improved the standard of living worldwide. Hunger is at its lowest level in human history. As Steven Pinker notes, "In the mid-19th century it took twenty-five men a full day to harvest and thresh a ton of grain; today one person operating a combine harvester can do it in six minutes."[5]

You are reading this book because of advances of science expressed through the printing press and, more recently, computer technology. You may have purchased your copy with a handheld device or a computer, both with greater computing power than the computer that propelled the Apollo 11 mission to the moon in 1969. The church would do well not to denigrate science and empirical evidence.

Relative to divine healing and deliverance, we also do well not to discard medical science and psychological insight. All knowledge is ultimately God's knowledge, and he delights in humanity discovering what he has created. As Proverbs 25:2 says, *"It is the glory of God to conceal a matter; to search out a matter is the glory of kings."*

---

[5] Steven Pinker, *Enlightenment Now: The Case for Reason, Science, Humanism and Progress* (New York: Viking, 2018), 75.

A PHYSICIAN'S STORY OF INTEGRATING DIVINE HEALING

I have been a physician for twenty-nine years, but my love of science started in childhood. Jesus and I go back as far as I can remember. I have never seen science and faith as incompatible but as intertwined and inseparable.

Six years ago, I went to a healing conference. I received a word of knowledge demonstrated by experiencing pain and numbness in my thigh with no apparent cause. When I shared it with the audience, a woman jumped up and said it was for her. The leader told me that I would be praying for healing for this woman. "Say what?!" I had no clue how to do that. As I started to pray, I asked Jesus to show me how. It was like an anatomy book opened in my mind—I could see this woman's leg and back and where things were not right. I prayed for those things to be healed, one at a time. And she was healed! She had had unremitting pain for seven years, and it was gone in a matter of minutes. It was a paradigm shift for me.

I then asked Jesus to teach me. He would nudge me at various times, in church, when out walking, on airplanes, with friends and strangers. When I stepped into that leading, I watched Jesus heal people. Then I started feeling these nudges at work, in my medical practice. Jesus always provides an opening as patients mention God or prayer. I jump all over that and offer to pray. One patient had neurologic symptoms after having surgery on her spine. When I offered to pray for healing, she grabbed my hand, put it on her back, and said, "pray here." As I prayed, her strength increased, and numbness decreased. She jumped up and walked across the room without her cane. Now when she comes in, we deal with her concerns, and then she tells me what she needs healing prayer for.

It was incredible watching Jesus move in this way, but he had more. After receiving inner healing and deliverance myself, I wanted others to experience the freedom and healing I had received. Jesus is teaching me more every day as I have the privilege of journeying with people in it. I had a patient who was tormented by the enemy. She saw dark figures and heard voices telling her to kill herself. She had been in the emergency room every 2–4 weeks with a suicide attempt for a couple of years, despite medication and therapy. When she comes in to see me, I bind the evil spirits and loose the Holy Spirit over her. Sometimes I get the opportunity to talk about Jesus and pray over her. When I do that, the emergency reports will stop, sometimes for extended periods. My hope is that she will come to know Jesus and receive the freedom He has for her.

Another patient had a long history of trauma, some at the hands of physicians. Our visits deal with some physical concerns, but mainly with the anxiety she has coming to my office and the physical, emotional, and spiritual trauma from her past. I spend a lot of time praying with her and speaking Jesus's truth over her. I suggested that she go through Soul Care *(Rob Reimer's book/course) with a friend. Towards the end of that journey, she was finally able to let me examine her. It was a huge step, even though it still required a lot of prayer and inviting Jesus into that space. I was then privileged to lead her through deliverance. She now walks closely with Jesus and her Heavenly Father (a first), despite her circumstances. I am watching the effects of the trauma unravel.*

With every healing and deliverance that I have been a part of, I am amazed at how Jesus meets each person with his incredible love, compassion, and power. This is beyond beautiful for me. I call this holistic medicine, and it is the kind of physician I want to be. As I watch Jesus bring freedom and healing, as people experience his love in action, I sit in awe of the great Physician, Jehovah Rapha.

With a full embrace of the natural, empirical sciences, let's turn our attention to the supernatural. Today in many churches in the West, the supernatural fingerprint of God is often difficult to observe. Many churches seldom, if ever, experience Jesus healing someone or freeing someone from demonic torment. Things weren't always this way. As we'll explore in Chapter 7, the first three hundred years of the church were profoundly characterized by the spoken and supernatural expression of the Gospel. The world recognized the people of God as being those who had the power to cure diseases and cast out demons. Then, for the better part of fifteen hundred years, the expression of healing and deliverance significantly fell off the map. We'll dive into this in Chapter 8.

TWENTY-FIRST CENTURY WORLDVIEW

The twenty-first-century environment is not only increasingly open to the supernatural but pursuant of it. A dramatic shift of acceptance is underway in the West, yet one might not pick up on this if they only follow mainstream media. As is the case with other periods of history, rarely do the intellectual elite correspond in worldview to the quiet masses.

Annette Hill, Professor of Media at the University of Westminster, UK, observed in her formal research project on accepting the paranormal that such belief is on a dramatic rise in the UK and America.[6] She cites that "...almost half of the British population, and two-thirds of American people claim to believe in some form of paranormal such as extrasensory perception, hauntings, and witchcraft."[7] In other words, in the twenty-first century West, to not believe in some form of paranormal and supernatural activity is a minority position.

Hill argues that because society has an intense fascination with the dead, this suggests a significant historical and contemporary narrative within cultures. She concludes that the paranormal is quickly becoming mainstream and has birthed entire industries

---

[6] Paranormal, as defined by Hill, is a broad category that includes the potential existence of demonic spirits but may be limited to other unexplainable experiences such as telepathy, angels and aliens.

[7] Annette Hill, *Paranormal Media: Audiences, Spirits and Magic in Popular Culture* (New York: Routledge, 2011), 1.

around paranormal experiences, including Halloween. The October 25, 2007 edition of *The Economist* suggests that Halloween may become the new Christmas with its skyrocketing sales.[8] With a rising number of American television shows and movies including characters with supernatural and paranormal powers, Hill argues that the paranormal is becoming mainstream in postmodernity. "The process of going mainstream creates a paradox. As paranormal beliefs become part of popular culture, the meaning of paranormal changes from something extraordinary to something more ordinary. Beliefs become lifestyle practices."[9] In popular culture in the West, the supernatural is quickly becoming natural. A new normal, if you will. Author Tara Isabella Burton expands on this,

> Wellness culture, with its implicit belief in a mysterious energy that runs through us all, has become a $4.2 trillion industry, half the size of the global health care market. Eclectic spiritual and magical practices—from astrology to tarot to yoga to crystals to sage cleansing to meditation—are now integral parts of millennial culture. Urban Outfitters sells spell books. Media outlets breathlessly report on each new fad—yoga, Reiki, psychics, erotic dinner parties—that purports to cultivate a sense of spiritual well-being or capacity for undistracted presence.[10]

Still, other research would corroborate Hill's conclusions. In 2014, *Sociological Research Online* reported that thirty percent of British adults had experienced at least one paranormal experience. Cited research indicated a rise in paranormal experience from

---

[8]   Hill, *Paranormal Media,* 38.

[9]   Hill, *Paranormal Media,* 64.

[10]   Tara Isabella Burton. *Strange Rites: New Religions for a Godless World* (New York: Public Affairs, 2020), 240.

twenty percent of the US adult population in 1975 to sixty percent in 1991.[11] In 2016, *Social Compass* cited Gallup polls showing that in the US belief in the devil increased from fifty-five percent in 1990 to seventy percent in 2004. In a 2007 Baylor Religion Survey, fifty-three percent of Americans responded affirmatively to the question, "Is it possible to be possessed?"[12]

Some may suggest that belief in the paranormal (including demons) is higher among people with corresponding religious beliefs or poorer socio-economic backgrounds. Tom W. Rice (Professor of Political Science, University of Northern Iowa) concluded that these aren't factors.[13] In other words, belief and experience in the paranormal are relatively consistent across socio-economic boundaries.

Why the dramatic shift in the past fifty years? In academia, this question is only beginning to be addressed. Within popular culture, however, signs of mainstream acceptance of paranormal experience are rapidly growing. The national Canadian newspaper, The Globe and Mail, ran an article in 2018 addressing this reality. They cite the Pew Forum on Religion and Public Life, concluding that as people increasingly leave their historical religious affiliation, they find themselves searching for spiritual alternatives. The alternatives, the article illustrates, include the paranormal, such as astrology.[14] Western society is becoming more accepting of paranormal belief, including demonic entities, albeit detached from the underpinnings of Judeo-Christian belief. Brian Stiller observes, "In a world taught

[11] Madeleine Castro; Roger Burrows; and Robin Wooffitt, "The Paranormal is (still) Normal: The Sociological Implications of a Survey of Paranormal Experiences in Great Britain." *Sociological Research Online*, vol. 19:3 (2014): 16.

[12] Guiseppe, Giordan and Adam Possamai, "The Over-policing of the Devil: A Sociology of Exorcism." *Social Compass*, vol. 63:4 (2016): 444-460.

[13] Tom W. Rice, "Believe It or Not: Religious and Other Paranormal Beliefs in the United States." *Journal for the Scientific Study of Religion* 42:1 (2003): 95-106.

[14] Gayle MacDonald, "The Age of Aquarius: Why More People Are Turning to Astrology for Answers," *The Globe and Mail*, March 15, 2018, accessed April 13, 2018, https://www.theglobeandmail.com.

by *Buffy the Vampire Slayer* and in which Lucifer has a self-named program on Netflix, a West that finds it hard to believe in God finds little problem believing in evil."[15]

EVIL, THE NEW GOOD

In the eyes of the shifting Western worldview, this belief in evil may no longer have an exclusively negative view. As one scholar, Robert Muchembled, argues:

> In worlds increasingly marked by hedonism, individualism and the pursuit of happiness, even constantly renewed pleasure, the devil has often acquired positive connotations. Not only has he ceased to exist as a terrifying external figure, he no longer even provokes a fear of the self, a dread of the inner demon, if only that of the psychoanalysts. He has become a marketing ploy, often used as a symbol of pleasure or well-being.[16]

It's not surprising, therefore, to come across articles such as one published by the BBC in June 2018, illustrating the use of Tarot cards as icons in fashion and entertainment. The article, citing University of Athabasca (Canada) sociologist Mike Sosteric, argues that in an age of instability (Brexit, Trump, etc.), people feel out of control and look to things like tarot for a sense of control. "According to Dr. Sosteric, many people find it hard to relate to traditional religions, which often carry patriarchal values, and are

---

[15]   Brian C., Stiller, *From Jerusalem to Timbuktu: A World Tour of the Spread of Christianity* (Downers Grove, Illinois: IVP Books, 2018), 143.

[16]   Robert, Muchembled, *A History of the Devil: From the Middle Ages to the Present* (Cambridge, UK: Polity Press, 2003), 228.

turning instead to alternative belief systems."[17] In March of 2018, the Canadian Broadcasting Company news agency ran a story as a letter written from a prostitute to her multiple clients. She describes her clients as having a "demon inside."[18] What has become an increasingly acceptable reference in society remains somewhat unfamiliar to much of the church in the West.

SUPERNATURAL—THE HOPE FOR THE CHURCH

In his book *The New Copernicans: Millennials and the Survival of the Church*, David John Seel Jr. argues that the great hope of the contemporary church is found in the desire within the millennial generation. This generation hungers for transcendent experiences in ordinary life. He suggests we need to follow in the footsteps of Copernicus, who began to conceptualize a model universe that placed the Sun rather than the Earth at the center. Such an idea was laughable yet eventually took hold. The primary view of the world changed. The New Copernicans are beginning to conceptualize reality not in opposition to empirical science, but also recognizing that science has its limitations in defining reality.

The Western world is quickly coming out of its coma of a scientific-materialist worldview. Despite its massive and enduring contributions, there is too much that science doesn't explain. The natural and supernatural need not and shouldn't compete. In past decades the church relegated ministries of healing, and especially deliverance, to the mission field in faraway lands. Today, these facets of the gospel are increasingly becoming the front door to faith. Indeed, the marriage of science and supernatural, theologically and

---

[17]   Didem Tali, "The Tarot Revival Thanks to Brexit, Trump and Dior," *British Broadcasting Corporation,* 17 June 2018, accessed 17 June 2018, http://bbc.com.

[18]   Tabatha Scott (pseudonym), "Dear Jeff: a former sex worker's letter to the clients she once knew." *Canadian Broadcasting Corporation News,* March 25, 2018, accessed July 3, 2018, http://cbc.ca/news.

experientially, may well be what the church was designed for, and what world now deeply hungers.

CHRIST-FOLLOWERS EXTEND HEALING IN A MUSLIM COUNTRY

Casting out demons, healing the sick, and the healing of deep psychological wounds. These are Biblical events we saw happen in our ministry. God took two very ordinary people, with very ordinary stories, and very ordinary gifts and worked through us for his glory and purpose.

Charlie was a stranger to us, but the brother of a new friend. Our little Bible study made up of pre-believers had been praying healing for him for a few weeks. Michel was finally able to visit our friend John and his brother Charlie at home to pray for him. A month after a tooth extraction gone bad, Charlie was close to death from infection; the side of his face was so swollen his eye was protruding. The entire family was present as Michel prayed. They were from another religion and understood Michel prayed in the name of Jesus. Desperate to see their brother healed, they agreed to allow his prayers. Michel prayed a short prayer of healing and left. The next day he received a call from John who excitedly exclaimed, after a month of pain and agony, Charlie was being healed in front of them. John shouted into the phone telling us pus was spewing from his eye-socket. We love how God left no room for speculation about the source of healing! Immediately, Charlie was significantly better, and within a week was mostly healed. The result of this healing was almost all the adult members of the family chose Christ; through them, many neighbours also heard the gospel.[19]

---

[19]   An excerpt from Ronald Brown, editor. *On Mission - Stories of those who went*, Vol 2. 2021. https://www.cmacan.org/resources/

PART TWO

THE EVIDENCE
OF HISTORY

CHAPTER FOUR

JESUS, HEALING, AND DELIVERANCE

And lead us not into temptation,
but deliver us from the evil one.

—Matthew 6:13

By the time of the first century AD, both Jewish and Hellenistic (Greek) cultures had a "… sharp smell of an invisible battle [hanging] over the religious and intellectual life." There were now unseen forces that needed to be contended with.[20] The story of the Exodus of the Jewish people from Egypt provided some context to the subject of magic and sorcery through Pharaoh's employment of magicians (Exodus 5-14). Yet, although the Jewish people believed in the existence of evil spirits that needed to be contended with, this belief was associated with magic and sorcery, which were strictly forbidden. Thus, and because demons are not part of Old Testament Jewish cosmology, we see little, if any, evidence of exorcism in the Old Testament.[21]

The practice of magic and sorcery were on the rise, as recorded in such literature as the *Greek Magical Papyri*. In general, magical

---

[20]   Peter Brown. *The World in Late Antiquity: AD 150-750* (London: Thames & Hudson, 1971), 53.

[21]   Du Toit, "Life in Obedience to the Torah."

practices were either rejected or not respected by the intellectual elite in both Judaism and Hellenistic culture. The historical record shows, however, that such practice was widespread throughout both cultures.[22] "Evidence supports the fact that magic was a force relied upon by many people from various strata of Greco-Roman society. And to be successful in magical power was no small accomplishment, even though the blueblood 'literati' would mock such ideas."[23]

It is within such an environment that the Gospel writers of the New Testament begin their record. To a world increasingly preoccupied and fearful of the presence of evil, the approach to this anxious situation demonstrated by Jesus was "good news."[24] His perspective, however, was markedly different. The world he entered saw a spiritual realm filled with warring demons (gods). In contrast, Jesus only saw one opposing kingdom, that of Satan, being utterly defeated by his life, death, resurrection, and ascension.[25]

Jesus entered first-century Palestine, a world that was deeply fearful of the dark spiritual realm. The religious elites did little to help the people understand or contend with this reality. They, like many today, opted for the supposed safety of a cognitive-only religiosity rather than a transformational faith. It is little wonder then that Jesus's message and ministry drew such attention; he was decidedly distinct in his approach. His mission was to bring experiential freedom for the prisoner, the captive, and the blind.

Jesus demonstrated the ministry of healing and deliverance powerfully in his earthly ministry. They were key marks of his coming Kingdom. Of the fifty-two miracles recorded in the

[22] Kee, *Medicine, Miracles, Magic*, 100.

[23] Wendy Cotter, *Miracles in Greco-Roman Antiquity* (London: Routledge, 1999). 176.

[24] Brown, *The World in Late Antiquity*, 54.

[25] Everett Ferguson, *Demonology of the Early Christian World* (Lewiston, New York: Edwin Mellen Press, 1984), 20.

Gospels, eighty percent involve both healing and exorcism, and fifteen percent are described exclusively as exorcisms.[26]

These sums don't include the numerous summaries of Jesus's ministry in terms of healing the sick and casting out demons.[27] These expressions of the gospel were considered by Jesus to be his core mission. In Luke 4 he quotes Isaiah 61, describing his calling as bringing good news to the poor, liberty to captives, sight to the blind, and liberty to the oppressed. These were predictable and immediate signs of the illegitimate kingdom of darkness being replaced with the Kingdom of God within people's lives.

The fact that Jesus was able to heal people of illness and injury was truly remarkable. The fact that Jesus was able to cast out demons was not. There existed an entire industry around the business of casting demons out of people. We see an example of this in Luke 9:49 when the disciples of Jesus observed others driving out demons.

We also see a failed attempt of "itinerant exorcisms" in the story of the Sons of Sceva (Acts 19). Other extrabiblical writings contain further detail on how these itinerants functioned.

Their tactics didn't demonstrate spiritual authority over darkness. Instead, upon payment, they attempted to negotiate or intimidate evil spirits, adjuring and compelling them to leave. Most frequently, the spirits would leave one person and enter another. It was a monetized business, very much like one might seek the services of a medical or wellness practitioner today.

THE DISTINCTIVENESS OF JESUS

The difference in Jesus's approach to deliverance is what drew such remarkable attention. His approach had four primary marks,

---

[26] See Appendix B for complete listing and categorization of Jesus's miracles, including exorcisms.

[27] I.e., Mt. 8:16, 9:34, Mk. 1:34, 1:39, 6:13.

all of which ought to characterize the ministry of deliverance in the church.

1. Authority. Jesus didn't attempt to intimidate, threaten, coerce or negotiate with demons. With his authoritative spoken word, he commanded their departure. No yelling needed.

2. Brevity. The attempts at deliverance by itinerant exorcists frequently involved hours or days. Jesus accomplished people's deliverance quickly, and often with merely a spoken word.

3. Selflessness. Jesus didn't demand money in exchange for service. Jesus's ultimate purpose was being well-expressed through the ministry of setting captives free, and free of charge!

4. Compassion. Jesus's focus was less on the demonic entity and more so on the person to whom he was ministering. He expressed genuine care and compassion to individuals, certainly not casting spirits out of one and into another.

Within this framework, what can we learn about Jesus and his approach to healing and deliverance from the four Gospels? In what ways does each gospel offer a unique perspective?

THE GOSPEL OF MATTHEW

In comparison to the Gospels of Mark and Luke, Matthew offers fewer accounts of healing and deliverance, yet he does include more summary accounts. An example is found in Matthew 8:16, which says, *"When evening came, many who were demon-possessed were brought to him, and he drove out the spirits with a word and healed all the sick."*

Matthew is less concerned with the details of how Jesus conducted his miracles as he is with demonstrating that Jesus was bringing the Kingdom of Heaven near. Healing and deliverance—that is the good news of an experienced gospel—therefore, are primary marks of this advancing Kingdom.

The good news is that a redeeming Kingdom of Light has come to replace the illegitimate kingdom of darkness. This advancing Kingdom frees all those who enter it from the curse of the kingdom of darkness.

Similarly, Jesus commissioned his disciples into this ministry, giving them his authority to drive out impure spirits and heal the sick (Matthew 10:1).

THE GOSPEL OF MARK

Mark describes the miraculous ministry of Jesus in greater detail than any other gospel. Nearly one-fifth of Mark's script is devoted to healing, exorcism, and the raising of the dead.[28] It is widely held that Mark's aim for writing was to inform the church what it means to be a disciple of Jesus. So prevalent are Mark's portrayals of exorcism that it is reasonable to conclude that he is attempting to illustrate the centrality of exorcism to the mission and message of Jesus and the subsequent followers of Jesus.

Mark's gospel was written distinctively to the early church, to train her in disciple-making and lay out standards and expected practices. As such, Mark recorded a wide variety of methods and approaches employed by Jesus in healing and deliverance. To some, Jesus touched them as he healed them. To others, he only spoke a word. Mark, more than Matthew or Luke, illustrates and demonstrates the breadth of tools the church can utilize in carrying on the mission of Jesus, in both its proclaimed and supernatural forms.

---

[28]   Daunton-Fear, *Healing in the Early Church*, 32.

For a contemporary church that frequently appears rather bankrupt in its ability to function in healing and deliverance, the words of historian Amanda Porterfield are both helpful and challenging. "Among all the activities ascribed to Jesus in the New Testament Gospels, exorcism and healing are among the most prominent."[29]

THE GOSPEL OF LUKE

Luke addressed a more sophisticated audience than his peers. In doing so, he frequently blurs the lines between the ministries of healing and deliverance. The terms are commonly used either together or interchangeably. Whereas Matthew didn't introduce the demonic realm until after the Sermon on the Mount, Luke (also Mark) leads with this early, and it emerges as a central theme.

Luke's overall perspective is framed in Luke 4. After his baptism, Jesus was immediately led by the Spirit into the wilderness for forty days, where the devil tested him. His ministry begins with this showdown. At the end of the forty days, Jesus appeared in the synagogue and read from Isaiah 61. In doing so, Jesus stated his mission.

> *The Spirit of the Lord is on me, because he has anointed me to proclaim good news to the poor. He has sent me to proclaim freedom for the prisoners and recovery of sight for the blind, to set the oppressed free, to proclaim the year of the Lord's favor.*
> —Isaiah 61:1–2

Following this, and still in chapter 4, Luke records the first miracle of Jesus, driving out an impure spirit from a man in the synagogue in Capernaum. This demonstrates Luke framing Jesus's

---

[29]   Amanda Porterfield, *Healing in the History of Christianity* (New York: Oxford University Press, 2005), 21.

ministry as the experiential realization that the curse is defeated, and freedom will now begin to reign.

Interestingly, Jesus's ministry of deliverance began within the religious environment of his day, within the synagogue. This ought to be noteworthy to the modern-day church as well, given that the enemy's work may well be covertly rooted in current leaders.

Luke is framing the showdown between the kingdom of darkness and the Kingdom of Light, with the latter proving victorious through the power of the Holy Spirit. Luke also seems to present that all sickness ultimately emerges from the kingdom of Satan, even though it may not have directly been caused by a demonic spirit (Luke 13:10-17).

THE GOSPEL OF JOHN

The Gospel of John doesn't contain an exorcism narrative, and there are remarkably few recorded healings compared to the other Gospels. John has a different purpose in his writing. He attempted to prove to his readers that Jesus is the Messiah, the Son of God (John 20:30-31).

As such, John's recorded miracles are less personal and more sovereign in nature. John's miraculous narratives focus more on Jesus's power over the natural realm, over death, and infinite empowerment (i.e., feeding the five thousand). John's message frequently refers to the miraculous ministry of Jesus as being "signs," a descriptor not utilized by the synoptic Gospels (Matthew, Mark, and Luke).

Contrary to what some suggest, John wasn't building a case for Jesus's ministry as being devoid of healing and deliverance. Instead, John's goal was to present a view of Jesus from more of a cosmological viewpoint, to ultimately reveal God's glory. John demonstrates that the kingdom of darkness is ultimately defeated by truth, truth as the person of Jesus.

Although perhaps not overtly expressed in his gospel, John provides an even more profound view of the effect of the kingdom of darkness upon the earth. His later writings provide this in vivid detail.

The reason the Son of God appeared was
to destroy the devil's work.

—1 John 3:8

We know that we are children of God, and that the whole world
is under the control of the evil one.

—1 Jn 5:19

MAUREEN RECEIVES PHYSICAL HEALING

A couple of years after my conversion into faith in Christ, I was beginning to learn more about physical healings like the Bible portrayed, as well as knowing people who were experiencing healing in their own lives. I was told by doctors that I had an anomaly in my lower back and pelvis, evidenced with the left leg shorter than the right, which would hinder me from carrying a child-to-term pregnancy.

Max Solbreken was an evangelist during those years with what we would call a healing ministry. We heard that Mr. Solbreken was holding a healing night in the town nearby, so we decided to make plans to go to the meeting and have him pray for my back. Some family members and I were seated in the auditorium with much anticipation since this was the first time we encountered this type of prayer. After teaching from scripture, he asked for anyone who wanted prayer for back problems to come up and stand by the side of the stage. I was one of a handful who came specifically for lower back issues. It was all very new and exciting!

It was my turn to believe God for a miracle. Max called me on stage and had me sit up very straight in a chair. He gently lifted both my legs so they were horizontal to the chair. Then he put my heels together, and it was very apparent that the left leg was about one and a half inches shorter than the right. He had his hands out, my heels resting gently on his palms. He did no pulling and knelt quietly at my feet. He had the audience take a good look at the very noticeable difference. He then asked me if I believed that Jesus could heal me, and I said with deep faith, "I do."

He began praying, and what happened next is hard to find words for, but I could physically feel my leg and pelvis moving! It moved like a gentle wave, from the left hip outward and then from my hip down to the bottom of my foot. I was actually aware that my leg was growing. There was no discomfort, just a sense of slight pressure and movement. I had my eyes closed, and I could hear the gasps and hallelujahs from the audience. He showed me the heels, which were now evenly placed together in his hands. Yes, my legs were now the same length, and I had experienced my first miracle!

He had me touch my toes and run around the auditorium. I did so with no pain or discomfort! Now I was the one shouting praises to Jesus as the others before me had done. For three days after this healing, there was a very hot heat radiating from my lower back. Many friends and family laid their hands on my back and were amazed at how hot it was. I was basking in a feeling somewhat like being suspended in the air for many days. I felt peace and love like I had never known and a sense of well-being that I will never forget.

That experience was the first of several physical healings the Lord would bestow upon me in the coming years. It drew me deeper into relationship with Father, Son, and Holy Spirit. It made me hungry for more of him and a deep longing for him in my soul. I was able, over the years, to carry three beautiful daughters to full-term pregnancy. Thank you, Jesus!

JESUS'S HANDOFF TO HIS FOLLOWERS

Christ's ministry proclaimed and dispensed freedom. This is a tangible demonstration of a compassionate, loving God, setting captives free from bondage and setting creation aright.[30] Within the bookends of scripture, Jesus's ministry of healing and deliverance is a picture of a loving God rescuing humanity from its hopeless entrapment by an abusive, destructive and illegitimate kingdom. From this viewpoint, Jesus commissioned his followers to preach the good news, proclaim the coming Kingdom, heal the sick, and cast out demons.

Curiously, while few in the Western evangelical church contest the notion that Jesus operated in the miraculous, many are either unsure or skeptical of the same being legitimate today. Inherent to this view is exegetical hypocrisy. As Dennis Hamm notes, "…it would not be honest to take literally language in the New Testament about a Holy Spirit (*pneuma hagion*) and to psychologize the language referring to an unclean spirit *(pneuma akatharta)*."[31]

Jesus's hand-off of the ministry of proclaiming, healing, and casting out of demons rings loudly throughout the Gospels and in particular, the Synoptic Gospels.

There are numerous accounts of Jesus commissioning his twelve disciples with his authority (*exousia*) to do the task of healing the sick and casting out demons (Mt. 10:1,8; Mk. 3:15; 6:7). The disciples returned from their short-term mission trips with joy and amazement. They too possessed the authority to advance this new Kingdom of God against the powers of darkness. This same authority (*exousia*) was extended beyond the twelve to the

---

[30] Graham H. Twelftree, *In the Name of Jesus: Exorcism among Early Christians* (Grand Rapids: Baker Academic Press, 2007), 128.

[31] Dennis Hamm, *The Ministry of Deliverance and the Biblical Data* (1980), quoted in Francis MacNutt, *Deliverance from Evil Spirits* (Grand Rapids: Baker Publishing, 2009), 45.

seventy-two, who enjoyed the same efficacy against the powers of darkness (Luke 10:1, 17-19).

The ultimate "hand-off" occurs in what has come to be known as "The Great Commission" in Matthew 28:16-20. In verse 18 Jesus declares that "...*all authority* (gk: exousia) in heaven and on earth has been given to me" (emphasis mine), and in doing so, he asserts his newly-purchased authority and his established Kingdom of Light over the kingdom of darkness through the church. In this sending out of the early church on mission, Jesus's hearers couldn't have understood his use of the word 'authority' (*exousia*) to have any application that didn't include, as its central expression, the proclamation of good news, the healing of the sick, and the casting out of demons. As Graham Twelftree asserts,

> The Great Commission, which is to be fulfilled in the narrative world of the readers, is to parallel the mission of Jesus. In other words, to answer the question about the intended audience for the commissioning instructions: Matthew intends the instructions of the commission for mission, including those related to exorcism, to apply to his readers."[32]

For the modern church to miss this connection is to fantastically misunderstand the mission of Jesus historically, let alone currently.

This dispensation of authority didn't come as a surprise to the early disciples. They had already been taught by Jesus that "...*whoever believes in me will do the works I have been doing, and they will do even greater things than these, because I am going to the Father*" (John 14:12). They recognized that they received the same 'sent-ness' by the Spirit that had been with Jesus (John 20:20). This empowerment would

---

[32]   Twelftree, *In the Name of Jesus,* 166.

come upon them as they waited in Jerusalem prior to their formal launch into their public ministry (Luke 24:38).

Chuck Davis compels Christ-followers today to walk in this same reality.

> We have been recruited to bring refreshed authority to a world that has gotten out of balance and thus is not experiencing God's fullest blessing and abundance. We live in a world with all types of competing authorities, powers, and dominions. Spiritual authority in Christ trumps all of these. As these powers come against us, we are to raise our spiritual hand and say "No!" As these powers block the advance of God's kingdom, we are to exert our authority as ambassadors to accomplish the king's rule.[33]

The church would do well to take seriously the words they pray in The Lord's Prayer, which clearly references Jesus's timeless ministry of deliverance, *"...lead us not into temptation, but deliver us from the evil one"* (Matthew 6:13). Some Bible translations omit the personal nature of the text with the phrase "deliver us from evil." However, a better and more defensible translation of the Greek renders it "deliver us from the evil one." A battle exists, and Jesus instructed his church to pray and extend his ministry of deliverance from darkness to his marvelous light.

---

[33] Chuck Davis, *The Bold Christian: Using Your God-Given Spiritual Authority as a Believer* (New York, NY: Beaufort Books, 2013), 59.

CHAPTER FIVE

THE NEW TESTAMENT CHURCH & DEMONIZED CHRISTIANS

*...that you may declare the praises of him who called you out of
darkness and into his wonderful light.*

—1 Peter 2:9

THE NEW TESTAMENT CHURCH

The newly-birthed church at Pentecost showed immediate evidence that Jesus's ministry of introducing the Kingdom was
intended to continue through his followers (Acts 2). They gathered in homes for worship, fellowship, and prayer. They immersed
themselves in the scriptures while walking in the baptism of the
Holy Spirit.

Among these things, what was predictable was proclaiming the
gospel, healing of the sick, and setting the oppressed free. With the
mission of Jesus still ringing in their ears, "Go and make disciples,"
they recognized that critical facets of disciple-making included the
working of signs and wonders such as healing and deliverance.

The first post-Pentecost story of healing is of the lame beg-
gar at the Beautiful Gate in Jerusalem in Acts 3. What is distinctive
about this healing, and the ones to follow, is that they were done
"In the name of Jesus." It was less so a formal ministry of the church

and more so expectant evidence of Jesus when he lights up the dark. Although supernatural empowerment was manifest through them, they recognized that Christ was the source of this power.

Further on in Acts, in response to emerging persecution, the early believers prayed for boldness in their message, "... *enable your servants to speak your word with great boldness. Stretch out your hand to heal and perform signs and wonders through the name of your holy servant Jesus*" (Acts 4:29-30). This young church saw little distinction between the message of the gospel and its predictable implications of healing and deliverance.

In Acts, we see the terminology shift slightly away from "healing" and "exorcism" to "signs and wonders." This shouldn't dissuade us because the bulk of signs and wonders expressed in the Gospels are healings and exorcisms. In Acts 4:30, the prayers and expectations of this newly birthed church, without doubt, included these same acts as primary expressions.

Additionally, when one looks at the signs and wonders recorded in Acts, there is ample evidence that healing and deliverance are part of the overall package.[34] Frequently, the author of Acts, Luke, uses "signs and wonders" as the descriptor, most notably found in Exodus, with Moses performing signs and wonders to free Israel from captivity. In his mind, Spirit-filled believers are now performing such wonders.

THE PERSPECTIVE OF PAUL

Some have suggested that Paul wrote little about exorcism and deliverance, that such miracles didn't characterize his ministry. However, one needs to look more carefully at his usage of terminology. He amply cited his belief in evil powers (1 Cor. 5:5; 7:5; 2 Cor. 2:10-11; 11:14-15; 1 Thes. 2:18). Specifically, Paul's language on

---

[34]   I.e., Acts 3:1-11, 5:12, 8:4-8, 19:11-12, 20:8-12, 28:7-9

the matter was extensively that of "signs and wonders," which again couldn't have been interpreted in any other way than healing and exorcism being primary expressions. In Romans 15:17-20, Paul describes his approach to apostolic ministry, and this is accompanied "…*by the power of signs and wonders, through the power of the Spirit of God*" (Romans 15:18). Such was the ministry of Paul, as seen in Acts, and many of his miracles included healings (Acts 14:8-12, 28:8), exorcisms (Acts 16:16-24, 19:13-16), and resurrections (9:36-41, 20:8-12).

The New Testament church carried on the ministry of bringing the freedom that Jesus inaugurated and commissioned. This was instrumental in the growth and rapid advance of the church. As Jesus's ministry was built upon miraculous signs, so was that of Paul.[35]

EXORCISM OR DELIVERANCE?

Let's pause here to address the question: what is the difference between exorcism and deliverance? This question can be answered in two ways, characteristically and historically.

The characteristics of exorcism and deliverance differ. While they both involve the expulsion of demonic spirits, their tactics aren't similar. An exorcist essentially adjures (urge and request) an evil spirit to leave. He or she may use a variety of external elements to do so, such as a Cross, recitations, and incantations. The exorcist attempts to intimidate or frustrate the demon to become uncomfortable and depart its current location. Negotiations with the demonic are not uncommon. This process is typically quite lengthy, can be very dramatic, and often exposes the exorcist to personal attack from the demonic forces (see the Sons of Sceva account in Acts 19).

Deliverance bears the marks of Jesus. The experience is comparatively brief, much less dramatic, and doesn't need to expose the

---

35   Twelftree, *In the Name of Jesus,* 66.

practitioner to peril. How is this accomplished? The person conducting the deliverance ministers under the protection of Jesus and utilizes the authority of Christ that is accessible to every believer. By mere command, demons submit and are expelled. It never ceases to amaze me how powerful Jesus is over darkness. His authority is absolute. Any sense of resistance offered by the demons in deliverance is merely through any grounds they may still have to be in the person's life, and that needs to be broken first.

Plainly stated, exorcism utilizes 'helps' external to the practitioner to intimidate the demon to leave. Deliverance uses the internal, Jesus-given authority to command demons to leave as the Holy Spirit directs. Every Christ-follower possesses this authority. They might not know how to utilize or appropriate it, but they do possess it.[36]

A historical perspective is also helpful to differentiate between exorcism and deliverance. In ancient literature, including scripture, only one term was used to encapsulate both, that is, exorcism. According to the above definitions, when Jesus or his followers functioned in deliverance, it might be described as exorcism. There was no other term to describe such ministry or function. The term deliverance didn't emerge broadly until the 20th Century as a distinction from the practice of exorcism. In the context of this book, the terms are used interchangeably depending on the historical context.

NON-APOSTLES AND THE SUPERNATURAL

Some have erroneously argued that signs and wonders were reserved for the apostles as part of the authentication of the holy scriptures

---

[36] For more on this topic see Chapter 4 of my previous book, *The Empowerment Pivot, How God is Redefining Our View of Normal*.

being written.[37] This view is biblically bankrupt. Miraculous signs of healing, deliverance, and other supernatural phenomenon are not the legitimatization of the canon of scripture. Instead, they are perpetual signs of the Kingdom of God coming near, typically expressed with compassion to individuals and groups.

Cessationists contend that supernatural ministry was limited to the category of apostles in the early church. The biblical evidence is in the opposite direction. In Galatians 3:5, Paul acknowledges that there were people among the Galatians church through whom the Spirit "works miracles," and these people wouldn't fall under the category of 'apostle.'

In Acts 8, we read of Philip the Evangelist, not to be confused with Philip the Apostle. His ministry was characterized by numerous exorcisms and physical healings (Acts 8:4-8). Stephen, also not an apostle, is described in Acts 6:8 as a man who "performed great wonders and signs." Beyond individuals, Paul describes the church in Galatia as a community where miracles were commonplace (Galatians 3:5).

A broad demonstration of supernatural authority given by Christ characterizes the New Testament Church. Ramsay Mac-Mullen, a scholar of early Christianity, cites this miraculous element as being a decisive factor in the advance of the early church: "Jesus, the apostles, and the early church conducted signs and wonders, and this produced conversions."[38]

---

[37] This theological position is known as *cessationism*. Cessationism is a term used to describe the bankrupt belief system that was developed within Protestantism that asserts that "... the purpose of miracles was to confirm the validity of revelation, and so, once the Bible was complete, all miracles ceased." *New Dictionary of Theology: Historical and Systematic*, 2nd ed., Downers Grove: IVP Academic, 2016), s.v. "Miracles," p. 579.

[38] Ramsay MacMullen, *Christianizing the Roman Empire (A.D. 100-400)* (New Haven: Yale Univ. Press,1984), 22.

CAN CHRISTIANS HAVE DEMONS?

An oft-asked question is whether or not believers can be possessed by demons. For some readers, it may be challenging to continue without clarifying this critical issue. Gratefully, the New Testament writings provide a solid foundation upon which to stand. To begin, to point-blank answer the question, "Can Christians be possessed?" My answer is an emphatic "no!" However, this is usually the wrong question. If the question is, "Can Christians be demonized?" My answer is an emphatic "yes!" as scripture argues only in this direction. This will, however, require some definition.

Understanding whether Christians can have demons comes down to three elements: 1) language, 2) biblical evidence, and 3) personal experience. First, language is essential. Many translations of the Bible translate the Greek word, *daimonizomai,* as 'possessed' in reference to Jesus and his disciples performing exorcisms (deliverance). This interpretation is unfortunate. The understanding of 'possession' in our day is primarily that of ownership. I.e., "we possess our house today" or, as the Merriam-Webster dictionary states, to be "influenced or controlled by something."

If one is a believer in Christ, they are indeed possessed; not by evil spirits but by the Holy Spirit! Jesus has purchased and redeemed them. His indwelling Spirit is an eternal deposit guaranteeing eternity in the Kingdom of God.

If you don't yet know Jesus, you can become a child of God through faith in Christ, and in doing so, you also become a residence for God's presence. He will surely light up the dark places in your life![39]

A more accurate English translation of *daimonizomai* is simply "demonized," which suggests that a person is "under the power

---

[39] For a good place to further explore faith in Jesus, check out www.iamsecond.com and www.christianityexplored.org.

of a demon"[40] or, as used in ancient extrabiblical literature, to be "tormented by a demon."[41]

There is much biblical evidence for Christian believers being demonized. Ephesians 4:27 warns against giving the devil *topos* (gk), which is translated as a foothold, ground, or opportunity.

> *"In your anger do not sin": Do not let the sun go down while you are still angry, and do not give the devil a foothold.*
>
> —Ephesians 4:26-27

The Greek word *topos* is where the English term topography emerges from. Commonly, people who function in deliverance refer to whether or not demons have "grounds" in a person's life. The demonic can only dwell where they have some legal right, so what might these legal grounds be? In Ephesians 4, the grounds Paul referred to was anger that could lead to sin. Other categories include unforgiveness, belief in lies about self or God, agreements with fear, unrepentant sin, trauma and abuse, participation in the occult, and so on.[42]

So how does this demonstrate that Christians can be demonized? Consider who the audience of Ephesians was: *"God's holy people in Ephesus, the faithful in Christ Jesus"* (Ephesians 1:1). Evidently, the enemy can gain some measure of influence, some ground, to torment a believer.

---

[40]   Joseph Henry Thayer, *Greek-English Lexicon of the New Testament* (Grand Rapids: Zondervan, 1972) 123.

[41]   Frederick W. Danker, Walter Bauer, and William F. Arndt, *A Greek-English lexicon of the New Testament and other early Christian literature* (Chicago: University of Chicago Press, 1979) 169.

[42]   For further study and equipping on this matter, see Rob Reimer's book *Soul Care: 7 Transformational Principles for a Healthy Soul*. Franklin, Tennessee. Carpenter's Son Publishing, 2016, and online experience, Soul Care (https://renewalinternational.org).

Later Paul exhorts his readers to *"Put on the whole armor of God, that you may be able to stand against the schemes of the devil"* (Eph. 6:11, ESV). Paul saw believers as candidates the devil could gain access to. Paul warns prospective elders against falling under the devil's condemnation or into the devil's schemes (1 Tim. 3:6,7), and again, this is written to Christians. To fall to such schemes of the enemy is to be demonized, suffering to some degree from the influence and impact of demonic presence.

James addresses this matter in James 4:7 when he exhorts the people of God to *"resist the devil,"* clearly implying that the devil moves against believers; passivity and naivety can lead them to fall prey to his influence. Earlier, James warned his readers against harboring bitterness and envy as such things have their source in the demonic:

> But if you harbor bitter envy and selfish ambition in your hearts, do not boast about it or deny the truth. Such "wisdom" does not come down from heaven but is earthly, unspiritual, demonic. For where you have envy and selfish ambition, there you find disorder and every evil practice.
>
> —James 3:14-16

Peter expands upon this when writing to *"the elect"* (1:1); he warns that *"Your adversary the devil prowls around like a roaring lion, seeking someone to devour. Resist him ..."* (1 Peter 5:8 ESV). Peter is aware that the enemy schemes to bring destruction to the life of the believer. How is it that many believers today question that Christians can be impacted negatively (demonized) by the devil?

Sadly, too many Christians erroneously believe that they can't be demonized and are thus more vulnerable to the enemy's schemes. The tragedy occurs on multiple levels, not the least of which is that the power of Christ is available; they can live free of demonic influence and harm. Further, only a minority of churches in the West properly disciple their people to understand this reality and equip them to walk in freedom and to set others free.

A PASTOR'S CHAINS ARE BROKEN

For much of my life, I have struggled with several persistent sin patterns. Nothing I did was working. I prayed for years to be able to overcome them with no success. I struggled with numerous dynamics continually, such as:

- *Fear, especially relating to evangelism. I would receive spikes of fear so strong it felt physically painful.*
- *Anger/rage issues.*
- *Constant spirals of feeling like a failure/useless. These were crippling as a pastor.*
- *I would have night terrors so fierce I would wake up screaming.*

I started working through the Soul Care *book by Rob Reimer, delving into some of the possible root issues. I was making some progress, but not as much as I hoped. Before I was able to finish the book, I attended a conference that Reimer was leading. After one of the sessions, I went to him to be prayed for, to see if he had a 'word' for why I couldn't overcome these issues. After a few questions, he told me I had a few demons, and we could deal with it tomorrow.*

Well, it turns out he was right. Over one hundred named demonic spirits were cast out between that session and a few follow-up sessions. It was simple, straightforward, non-sensational. He would ask any evil spirits present in me some questions; I would report what I heard a voice inside saying. I was surprised when numerous witchcraft-type spirits emerged. I had no knowledge of any family history in witchcraft. Still, later, when talking with my grandmother, I was informed that there was actually a long line of intense witchcraft in the family. After getting what information was needed, Reimer would command the evil spirits to leave in Jesus's name.

Afterward, when hands were placed on me for prayer, I felt overwhelmed with love and peace, and for the first time felt I heard the inward witness of the Spirit (Rom 5:5, 8:15-16), an emotional wave and whispers of love and truth from scripture. I wept.

There has been a literal overnight transformation in my character since then. The following are in no particular order but represent the transformation I have experienced:

- Condemning thoughts are basically gone. No more cycles of "You're useless; you're a failure."
- Suicidal thoughts are gone.
- Night terrors are gone.
- The massive spikes of fear and anxiety have been dramatically reduced; they're human-sized now! I was finally able to lead someone to the Lord recently too!
- The nature of my struggle against lust has transformed. Much of the battle is gone.
- Rage is no longer instantaneous and explosive. Controlling my anger feels possible now, and many times there is no trace of the old anger.
- When praying to the Father, peace washes over my soul. Previously, I would feel no change when praying to him, or the anxiousness would get worse. Not anymore!
- My capacity for love and compassion has been greatly enlarged, especially with my children! I feel love for them now. My emotional numbness has been healed.
- My ability to hear God's voice has been dramatically increased. God's peace is so much better. He is so good. Praise God!
- There is, what I can best describe, a quietness in my soul. It feels like the buzz of dozens of voices has been silenced in my

*head. I wasn't even aware of them before, but I am deeply
aware of their absence.*

· *I am not afraid to be alone anymore. God's peace is so much
better. It feels like the weight of a dozen chains has been broken off my soul.*

The Gospels and the letters in the New Testament present a clear
picture of the Kingdom of Light pitted against the kingdom of
darkness. There is a battle. The ultimate victory is ensured. Believers must walk in their Jesus-purchased authority and the holiness
of Christ to ensure victory in the many battles along the way. In
this, there needn't be any sense of fear, for the enemy has no power
against Jesus nor his followers who walk in the light.

There are other passages that could be considered here, however, establishing the idea that Christians can be demonized wasn't
a high priority for the biblical writers: this wasn't questioned in
their day. For example, the early church prioritized deliverance
as part of the disciple-making process as common practice. They
were committed to new believers experiencing freedom through
healing and deliverance right away.

We will look further into this in the next chapter. It wasn't
until the post-Reformation and The Enlightenment period when
the Western Christian world no longer subscribed to the idea that
believers could be impacted significantly by demons.

CHAPTER SIX

THE EARLY CHURCH

For God, who said, "Let light shine out of darkness," made his light shine in our hearts to give us the light of the knowledge of God's glory displayed in the face of Christ.

—2 Corinthians 4:6

Have you ever wondered what the early church looked like; how they did or didn't carry on the miraculous ministry of Jesus and the apostles? Did these ministries continue, or did they cease? Were they exclusively done by church leaders or was this extended to the church at large? What did disciple-making look like? What might we learn from the early Christians?

The writings of the Church Fathers represent the roughly two-hundred-fifty-year period between the last of the apostles and the time of the Roman Empire adopting Christianity. In their writings, we find that the ministries of healing and deliverance were commonplace, diverse in expression, integrated with baptism, and focused upon the person of Jesus.

Contrary to the perspective of modern Cessationists, the ancient record is rich, documenting both the place and centrality of signs and wonders in the ministry of the early church, and specifically noting that of healing and casting out demons.

The worldview of the second-century Greco-Roman world was quite demon-conscience.[43] However, they didn't necessarily associate demons with a battle between good evil; rather, demons were viewed within the system and structure of gods who must be appeased.[44] Magic was common among the masses yet not as quickly recognized by the intellectual elite. From a popular perspective, any person who could master the world of magic and the realm of spirits would be accomplishing no small task. They would demand broad attention and enjoy the opportunity to monetize their skills.[45]

Let's look at some examples of writings from a limited sample of Church Fathers, who illustrate the practice of healing and deliverance in the early church.

JUSTIN MARTYR (100-165 CE)

Among the earliest recorded church fathers[46] is Justin Martyr, who spent his life in Asia Minor, Greece, and Rome. He had much to say on exorcism, and he described many believers performing exorcisms and healings:

> For numberless demoniacs throughout the whole world, and in your city, many of our Christian men exorcising them in the name of Jesus Christ, who was crucified under Pontius Pilate, have healed and do heal, rendering helpless and driving the possessing devils out of the men, though

---

[43] Ferguson, *Demonology of the Early Christian World*, 129.

[44] Daunton-Fear, *Healing in the Early Church*, 161-2.

[45] Cotter, *Miracles in Greco-Roman Antiquity*, 176.

[46] Much of the framework and material sourced in this chapter is derived from the historical overview in Frank C. Darling, *Biblical Healing: Hebrew and Christian Roots* (Boulder, Colorado: Vista Publications, 1989).

they could not be cured by all the other exorcists, and those who used incantations and drugs (*Second Apology* 6).

This depiction conveys something of an everyday experience within the church, whereby many believers were advancing the gospel utilizing the tools of deliverance and healing. He goes on to describe the supremacy of the name of Jesus over demons.

For every demon, when exorcised in the name of this very Son of God—who is the Firstborn of every creature, who became man by the Virgin, who suffered, and was crucified under Pontius by your nation, and died, who rose from the dead, and ascended into heaven—is overcome and subdued (*Dialogue with Trypho*, 85).

Justin saw the schemes of the enemy having application against both the faithful and the faithless, or, in other words, against believers and nonbelievers. He recognized the role of spiritual warfare as part of the church's evangelistic responsibility, to push back the enemy's schemes so that the unbeliever might see their way to faith in Christ.

But since the adversary does not cease to resist many, and uses many and divers arts to ensnare them, that he may seduce the faithful from their faith, and that he may prevent the faithless from believing, it seems to me necessary that we also, being armed with the invulnerable doctrines of the faith, do battle against him in behalf of the weak (*On the Resurrection*, 1).

New Testament scholar Graham Twelftree concludes that Justin "... probably considered exorcism to be not only the most important but also the most common form of Christian healing [and]… the most important weapon of evangelism Christians possessed…. Not surprisingly then, exorcism was the most common form of healing in which Christians were involved."[47]

IRENAEUS (120-200 CE)

Irenaeus, served as bishop in Lyons (present-day France); he saw prophecy, healing, exorcism, and even resurrections demonstrated by a wide variety of people. This had the effect of propelling evangelism, enabling the expansion of the church. He wrote the following some sixty to eighty years after the last of the apostles had died, noting the role of signs and wonders in many coming to faith in Christ:

> For some do certainly and truly drive out devils, so that those who have been thus cleansed from evil spirits frequently both believe and join themselves to the Church. Others have foreknowledge to things to come: they see visions, and utter prophetic expressions. Others still, heal the sick by laying their hands upon them, and they are made whole. Yea, moreover, as I have said, the dead even have been raised up, and remained among us for many years (*Against Heresies*, 2.32).

TERTULLIAN (145-220)

Tertullian lived much of his life in Rome, spilling much ink to defend both the supernatural ministry of Jesus about healing and exorcism as well as the supernatural ministry of his contemporary

---

47   Twelftree, *In the Name of Jesus,* 242.

church.[48] He saw exorcisms as a primary defense and apologetic as a response to those skeptical of the ministry of Jesus and as part of the standard calling of every believer.

> What nobler than to tread under-foot the gods of the nations—to exorcise evil spirits—to perform cures—to seek divine revealings—to live to God? These are the pleasures, these the spectacles that befit Christian men— holy, everlasting, free. (*The Shows*, XXIX)

Tertullian was remarkably confident of the centrality of the ministry of exorcism and its accessibility to every Christian. On one occasion, he dared his critics to bring the demonized to court and have a Christian confront and defeat the demon and if the Christian was not able, "…then and there shed the blood of that most impudent follower of Christ" (*Apology*, XXIII). In other words, Tertullian understood that every Christian had the ability to cast out demons, and if they were unable to, their faith was suspect. Although he may have been given to overstatement, Tertullian certainly believed that such ministry was not to be sequestered to the clergy class.

ORIGEN (185-254 CE)

Origen, living in Alexandria and Caesarea, wrote a rebuttal to Celsus, a critic of Christianity, entitled *Against Celsus*. Accusations were made of Christians casting out demons. Notably, Celsus didn't deny this but instead affirmed the Christian's ability to perform miracles and exorcise demons. However, he asserted that Christians were doing this through magical sources rather than

---

[48]   Darling, *Biblical Healing: Hebrew and Christian Roots*, 122-5.

the authority of Jesus.[49] Origin contended that through exorcism, "...many have been converted to Christianity... (1.46)." Of note is Origin's description of predictable outcomes that were experienced by those whom Jesus had delivered from demons.

> ... the name of Jesus can still remove distractions from the minds of men, and expel demons, and also take away diseases; and produce a marvelous meekness of spirit and complete change of character, and a humanity, a goodness, and gentleness in those individuals... (1.47).

Some modern-day historians, such as Ramsay MacMullen, contend that "...exorcism, possibly [was] the most highly rated activity of the early Christian church."[50] Other scholars contest this firm and highly exclusive conclusion but agree that the role of exorcism was a significant factor in the rapid expansion of the early church.[51]

Based on the ancient literature, such findings fly in the face of what is taught in many Christian circles today. Too frequently, the significant growth of the early church is attributed primarily to their hospitality and graciousness. Indeed, these elements were present in the early church. It was marked with love and hospitality towards those in and outside the church. However, the ancient record is conclusive: among the primary vehicles by which the early church expanded, there most certainly was the recognition that ordinary Christians had the ability to heal and had power over dark forces.

Conversions to Christian faith stemming from exorcisms are noted in the ancient literature from various locations such as Ephesus, Palestine, Italy, Africa, and Gaul.[52] Craig S. Keener states, "Be-

---

49   Darling, *Biblical Healing: Hebrew and Christian Roots,* 269.

50   MacMullen, *Christianizing the Roman Empire,* 27.

51   Twelftree, *In the Name of Jesus,* 26.

52   MacMullen, *Christianizing the Roman Empire,* 28.

fore the 300s, exorcisms proved to be a major factor in the spread of Christianity; in the 300s, exorcisms and miracles are the most explicit cause of conversion to Christianity mentioned in early Christian sources."[53]

DELIVERANCE, DISCIPLE-MAKING, AND BAPTISM

By the early/mid-second century, evidence emerged of exorcism being utilized as an evangelistic vehicle and a necessary element in the disciple-making process via pre-baptismal rites. Early church historian, S.V. MacCasland, argues that exorcism formed "perhaps the outstanding mark of discipleship in the early church."[54] One can't make gross generalizations of the pre-Nicaean church (325 CE). However, despite its geographic diversity, we see in the *Apostolic Tradition* (circa 215) a well-developed exorcism ritual " ... incorporated as an essential element of the baptismal process in the mainstream Christian Church."[55] So highly regarded were the sanctified waters of baptism that the church wished baptismal candidates to be purged from demonic powers before entering, believing the waters also had the power to expel any remaining demons.

Early Christians possessed a worldview of people moving from the kingdom of darkness into the Kingdom of Light, and this required cleansing and exorcising. Justin saw people's souls as swarming with devils prior to water baptism.[56] Origin equated the baptismal experience with that of the people of Israel escaping the hand of Pharaoh and seeing their enemies defeated in the waters.

---

53   Keener, *Miracles: The Credibility of the New Testament Accounts,* vol. 1, 362.

54   S.V. MacCasland, *By the Finger of God: Demon Possession and Exorcism in Early Christianity in Light of Modern Views of Mental Illness* (New York: MacMillian, 1951), 104, quoted by Porterfield, *Healing in the History of Christianity*, 62.

55   Elizabeth Leeper, "From Alexandria to Rome: The Valentinian Connection to the Incorporation of Exorcism as a Pre-baptismal Rite," *Vigiliae Christianae,* 44 (1990): 6.

56   J.N.D. Kelly, *Early Christian Doctrines* (San Francisco: Harper & Row, 1978), 167.

When, however, they come to the water of salvation and
to the sanctification of baptism, we ought to know and
to trust that there the devil is beaten down and the man,
dedicated to God, is set free by the divine mercy. For as
scorpions and serpents, which prevail on the dry ground,
when cast into water, cannot prevail nor retain their ven-
om; so also the wicked spirits, which are called scorpions
and serpents, and yet are trodden under foot by us, by the
power given by the Lord, cannot remain any longer in
the body of a man in whom, baptized and sanctified, the
Holy Spirit is beginning to dwell (*Epistle,* 75:15).

Cyprian (210-258 CE), serving as Bishop of Carthage in
North Africa, wrote extensively on the role of baptism in the life
of the believer, seeing the event as being instrumental in freeing a
person from the attachment of demonic spirits.[57]

But if anyone is moved by this, that some of those who
are baptized in sickness are still tempted by unclean spirits, let him know that the obstinate wickedness of the
devil prevails even up to the saving water, but that in baptism it loses all the poison of his wickedness... this also is
done in the present day, in that the devil is scourged, and
burned and tortured by exorcists, by the human voice,
and by divine power.... When, however they come to
the water of salvation and to the sanctification of baptism, we ought to know and to trust that there the devil
is beaten down, and the man, dedicated to God, is set free
by divine mercy (*Epistles LXXV,* 15).

---

57   Darling, *Biblical Healing: Hebrew and Christian Roots,* 143.

Cyprian explains how devils can return to a person after they have been exorcized through baptism if the person doesn't remain faithful.

> And, on the other hand, some of those who are baptized in health, if subsequently they begin to sin, are shaken by the return of the unclean spirit, so that it is manifest that the devil is driven out in baptism by the faith of the believer and returns if the faith afterwards shall fail (*Epistles LXXV*, 15).

As the pre-Nicene[58] church reached the third century, her personality and approach to the surrounding culture were firmly established, albeit with regional nuances. Although the writings that cite healing and deliverance are few compared to the overall volume of literature, they carry a clear message about the ubiquitous nature of these ministries. Couched in the larger bodies of literature, these citations show a vibrant picture that, while the early church was effective in healing and deliverance, their focus was on the person of Jesus. Historian Peter Brown summarizes the everyday experience of the church in this era:

> The Christians were convinced that they were merely 'mopping-up', on earth, a battle that had already been won for them in Heaven. The monks treated the demons with the delighted alarm of small boys visiting a lion in the zoo; and the Christian bishops set about their work in the heady frame of mind of many a revolutionary—they faced a diabolically organized society that was, at one

---

[58] The Nicene Creed was established in 325 A.D.

and the same time, towering, noxious, and yet hollow, doomed to destruction."[59]

A great measure of modern so-called scholarship completely disregards the supernatural evidence and depiction of the early church, relegating its growth to a mere sociological phenomenon. Not only is this a disservice to the early Christian witness but also to the ancient literature, writing from a non-Christian perspective. Certainly there were a variety of factors that led to the expansion of the early church. However, any student of history should be highly suspect of historians that downplay or dismiss the supernatural expression of the early church. This is little more than modern hubris. Brown elaborates on this,

However many sound social and cultural reasons the historian may find for the expansion of the Christian Church, the fact remains that in all Christian literature from the New Testament onwards, the Christian missionaries advanced principally by revealing the bankruptcy of men's invisible enemies, the demons, through exorcism and miracles of healings.[60]

WHAT CAN WE LEARN FROM THE EARLY CHURCH?

What can we learn from the early Christians? What of their experience might help us move closer towards Jesus's ultimate intention? Six things emerge at the top of the list. One, healing and deliverance were widespread throughout the known world and demonstrated by ordinary believers. Two, while some in the church might have functioned as equippers in healing and deliverance, it was recognized that all believers had the freedom to operate in these ministries. Three, although the church was proficient in healing and

---

[59]   Brown, *The World in Late Antiquity: AD 150-750*, 55.

[60]   Brown, *The World in Late Antiquity: AD 150-750*, 55.

deliverance, the focus of their attention was on the person of Jesus and not the presence of darkness. Four, deliverance was seen as an early and necessary step in the disciple-making process prior to water baptism. Five, healing and deliverance were among the primary vehicles toward the mass expansion of the church. The church was seen as having ability over sickness and darkness where other pagan practitioners had failed. Six, although methodologies differed regionally, what is common is that these miracles were performed "In the name of Jesus" with ascription given to Christ as the source of power and authority.[61]

FINDING JESUS THROUGH DELIVERANCE

J was desperate! His girlfriend M was not only acting strange, she was a completely different person. Not in the same way that you would describe someone who was depressed or angry. She was convulsing and screaming, her eyes would go dark, and she would say horrible things. He had called her mother, who had taken her to the hospital, hoping to find out what was wrong. He also called his two bosses—a couple in our church, who were also like a second father and mother.

Neither J nor his girlfriend were believers in Jesus. Their exposure to Jesus, the church, and the Bible were virtually non-existent except for the love and witness of this couple. The "mom" called me (Scott) to ask if my associate pastor and I could see her (not knowing she was already at the hospital). We went to the house of M's mother, only to be told that J and M were at the hospital, so we rushed over there.

We found J near the hospital's front doors, worried for M, panicked about what was going on, and scared by the things he had seen and heard. He

---

61   Larry W. Hurtado, "The Ritual Use Of Jesus's Name," in *Healing and Exorcism in Second Temple Judaism and Early Christianity*, ed. Michael Tellbe & Tommy Wasserman, (Tubingen Germany: Mohr Siebeck, 2019), 147.

asked me what was going on, and my associate pastor and I calmly explained the reality of the two kingdoms at war—God's kingdom and Satan's. It was a great way to introduce him to the gospel—the love, forgiveness, and power of Jesus Christ! It was clear that he believed what we were saying because he said he experienced peace as we were sharing, and it made sense of the demonic manifestations his girlfriend was having.

What he thought was a psychological issue was actually a deep and dark spiritual issue. He believed the gospel and accepted Christ on the spot! M was inside, under heavy sedation to control her convulsions (manifestations). J asked if we could help her, and we said we would do our best. He called the next day when she was released, and we went to the home where they lived together. We prayed to start our time together, and the evil spirits manifested immediately through contorting her body and screaming. We commanded the evil spirits to be still and silent, and with persistence, they calmed down under our authority in Christ. M was in pain and distress and asked if we could help her. We told her the same things we had told J the day before, that she needed to be a daughter in the kingdom of Jesus in order to experience the victory of Jesus over evil. She understood and accepted Jesus right away. Immediately she began convulsing again and screaming. Only this time, with her as a part of God's kingdom, our authority over the evil spirits was stronger and more effective because she belonged to Christ!

We commanded the demons manifesting to reveal their legal grounds for tormenting M. Through a process of eliminating their right to torment M, the evil spirits were evicted, and M experienced instant relief. The evil spirits had left, and in their absence, M was able to experience God's love and presence for the first time as a born-again believer! Under the love and presence of Jesus, she and J began reading a bible we had given them, stopped taking drugs (which turned out to be one of the primary legal grounds for the evil spirits to infest M's soul), and began growing in their faith. It was a great experience to see how deliverance ministry can actually be a pathway for sharing the gospel!

CHAPTER SEVEN

A LONG AND PRECIPITOUS DECLINE

*I am sending you to them to open their eyes and turn them from
darkness to light, and from the power of Satan to God....*

—Jesus (Acts 26:17-18)

I toyed with utilizing a pun in the naming of this chapter, "What
the Hell Happened?" Indeed, what did happen between the
first few centuries of the Church and the past one hundred years?
Healing and deliverance formed primary vehicles towards early
church expansion. However, the same ministries are nearly impossible to observe in most modern churches in the West. How
did something so central become so scarce in expression? The decline was long and precipitous but has clear explanations to its
cause and disintegration, along with crucial lessons for the present-day Church to capture.[62]

---

[62] I recognize this chapter is a rapid and somewhat shallow flyover of a lengthy and
complex period. What I offer here is intended to be more of general summary
observations and not an in-depth and academically rigorous presentation. For the
latter I commend the reader to both my citations and bibliography for more in-
depth analysis.

EARLY ROMAN CATHOLICISM

With the Edict of Milan by Roman Emperor Constantine in AD 313, Christianity became a legalized religion. The implications were, and continue to be, enormous. Instead of being a grass-roots, lay-empowered movement, the Church quickly became an organized religion with the trappings of institutional power. In the post-Constantine period, the Church gradually evolved from a movement of empowered disciples of Jesus to an organization, with centralized authority within the soon-to-be-established Roman Catholic Church.

With church hierarchy comes a desire to consolidate power; authority becomes isolated, limited to a small number of people. This contrasts with the early-church model of empowering and releasing ministry to all believers. With the ministries of healing and deliverance *intrinsically* demonstrating power and authority, they quickly became captured by the religious elite. Before long, the role of exorcist became limited to professional clergy and, specifically, bishops. Clergy climbing the organizational ladder would frequently be assigned the role of exorcist as a stepping-stone to more significant offices of the Church. The ministry of exorcism moved towards rote-ritual and was sequestered to an ecclesiastical position, away from demonstrating the spiritual authority in Christ that is accessible to all disciples.[63] Although exorcism continues in the historical record in the hundred years post-Constantine, it quickly becomes muted and sporadic.

THE MEDIEVAL PERIOD

The centralization of spiritual authority to the clergy class rather than all believers harmed the medieval Church. The European

---

[63]   Daunton-Fear, *Healing in the Early Church,* 151.

medieval period was characterized by a worldview of a great cosmic struggle between "good and evil, saints and devils, God and Satan."[64] This had enormous ramifications on the day-to-day affairs of ordinary people. Although miracles and exorcisms persisted, they were attributed to dead saints and a handful of individuals rather than living believers with the authority of Christ. Any miracles demonstrated through the Church, real or perceived, weren't generally seen as the work of Jesus as a demonstration of his kindness and coming Kingdom, but rather the exercise of magical powers, frequently syncretized with the local pagan belief systems.

Despite this unfortunate development, there were some bright spots in the period. Geographically one can observe that wherever fruitful evangelism was demonstrated, the accompaniment of miraculous signs often occurred. This can be seen with early medieval missionaries such as Augustine of Canterbury, Columba, missionary to Scotland, and Boniface to Germany.[65]

Exorcism as a pre-baptismal ritual became embedded in Roman Catholicism throughout the first millennium. This shouldn't be confused with effective, meaningful deliverance in disciple-making. Exorcism became highly ritualized with prescribed words spoken over the baptized infant.[66]

Belief in demons and the tangible effects of personified evil proliferated during the medieval period. So did a high measure of syncretism[67] between Christianity and local, traditional pagan

---

[64] Elmo Nauman, *Exorcism Through the Ages* (New York: Philosophical Library, 1974), 74.

[65] Keener, *Miracles: The Credibility of the New Testament Accounts,* 367.

[66] Bodo Nischan, "The Exorcism Controversy and Baptism in the Late Reformation," *The Sixteenth Century Journal, vol. 4, no. 1 (Spring 1987): 32.*

[67] Definition of 'syncretism,'—"The attempt to combine different or opposing doctrines and practices, esp. in reference to philosophical and religious systems." From *The Oxford Dictionary of the Christian Church,* 3rd edition revised. Edited by F.L. Cross & E.A. Livingston. Oxford: Oxford University Press, 2005, p. 1579.

religion. The impact of this provided the downward slope where exorcism and healing, where present at all, gravitated towards an association with magic, ritual, superstition, prayer to the saints, relics, and pilgrimages to holy sites, etc.[68] Very little remained of the authority of Christ given to the believer, the place of healing and deliverance in disciple-making. Gone were the hallmarks of the time of the Gospels, Acts, and the Early Church.

THE REFORMATION

The next historical shift had profound implications upon healing and deliverance for the modern Western Church, the Reformation. Beginning in the sixteenth century, reformers such as Luther, Calvin, and others, contributed much to the evolution of the Church. They restored the view of the authority of the Bible over papal dictate. They reintroduced the concept of the priesthood of all believers. They reasserted the doctrine that salvation is found in Christ alone. However, on supernatural matters, i.e., healing, deliverance, they did us no favors. Instead, they further entrenched their Church's trajectory away from a biblical, supernatural worldview. Both Luther and Calvin were theologians in the stream of Augustine. As such, they valued intellectualism at the expense of the supernatural. They positioned cognitive, theological understanding highly above experiential faith rather than seeing them as integrated and even complementary.

To their defense, they were reacting to the predominantly superstitious view of healing and exorcism in their era, which needed to be reformed. In their day, supernatural activities were highly connected to the pagan rites and rituals surrounding the Roman Catholic church through relics, shrines, and dead saints as mediaries.[69] The

---

68   Keener, *Miracles: The Credibility of the New Testament Accounts,* 269.

69   Porterfield, *Healing in the History of Christianity,* 24.

exchange of money frequently conducted these rites and rituals; in other words, these ministries were highly monetized.

Both Luther and Calvin taught that miracles are often the work of the devil, which formed part of their critique of the papacy.[70] Many scholars argue that Luther and Calvin's opposition to the miraculous "served their immediate polemical situation against Catholic apologetic use of miracle claims."[71] They were trying to take down the authority of the Pope. If the Pope claimed supernatural function, then to undermine the supernatural would serve to undermine the Pope. The primary battleground of the Protestant Reformation was questioning the source of authority; therefore, any claim of authority made by the Catholic Church, especially that which was linked to the so-called miraculous, was an easy target for the reformers.[72]

Luther and Calvin recognized that the Gospels are full of miracles. However, they needed to discount the supernatural as being available in their day (and thus discredit papal authority). Thus, they created a theological framework dispelling the work of the supernatural following the apostolic era. Calvin argued that miracles were primarily instruments to authenticate the original preaching of the Gospel. Luther believed that miracles were conduits of the formation of the Bible so that the people of God could get on with doing *"...greater works than these"* (John 14:12, ESV), such as teaching and converting souls.[73]

Again, to their defense, there was much that needed to be reformed. However, instead of reforming the approach to healing and exorcism in the Catholic Church, they choose to be essentially

---

[70]   Jane Shaw, *Miracles in Enlightenment England* (New Haven Connecticut: Yale University Press, 2006), 24-5.

[71]   Keener, *Miracles: The Credibility of the New Testament Accounts,* 374.

[72]   Shaw, *Miracles in Enlightenment England,* 23.

[73]   Keener, *Miracles: The Credibility of the New Testament Accounts,* 221.

silent on the matter. Regrettably, it is with these reformers that the doctrine of "cessationism" found its roots; the misguided and biblically-bankrupt belief that God's working of miracles through the Church ceased at the end of the age of the Apostles.

The Protestant Reformation essentially rendered the practices of healing and deliverance either forbidden or moot.[74] Reformers such as Calvin and Zwingli condemned the practice. They failed to recognize its roots in the early Church and tragically ascribed it as a "papal relic" and even "papal-magic" that needed to be done away with. Luther was slightly more tolerant, allowing it to be retained as part of the sacramental infant baptismal ceremony.[75] Notably, towards the end of his life, Luther shifted from his view on cessationism and was open to the healing work of Christ.[76]

Morton Kelsey observes that the Protestant reformers adjusted faith and practice in the Church but failed to reform the underpinnings of a failed worldview, and this continues to exist today. "The Protestant reformation changed many aspects of church life and practice, but it never attacked the problem of the world view of the [intellectuals] against whom it revolted. Among Protestants, this has not changed much since."[77] It can easily be argued that contemporary belief in cessationism (in theology or practice) can find its roots in the battle lines drawn a half millennia ago during the Reformation.

Over the following five hundred years, Protestant movements and denominations multiplied rapidly. Until the twentieth century, very few movements invested in extensive written theological

---

[74]   Bodo Nischan, "The Exorcism Controversy and Baptism in the Late Reformation," 31-51.

[75]   Porterfield, *Healing in the History of Christianity*, 33.

[76]   Robert Webster, *Methodism and the Miraculous: John Wesley's Idea of the Supernatural and the Identification of Methodists in the Eighteenth-Century* (Lexington, Kentucky: Emeth Press, 2013), 169.

[77]   Kelsey, *Healing and Christianity*, 220.

commentaries. Instead, most new movements relied heavily upon the writings of Luther and Calvin, and some still do today. As a result, cessationism continued to flourish and continued to remove much of Protestant Christianity from the supernatural work of Christ.

However, such a theological position didn't serve to completely halt the expression of the miraculous within pockets of the Church. In the fifteenth through seventeenth centuries, miracles of healing and exorcisms are noted within various streams of the Church; Puritans,[78] Anabaptists, Quakers, and Pietists, to name a few.[79] The expanse of these movements proved a threat to the more established and institutionalized Church. For example, in an attempt to suppress Puritanism, the Church of England took the formal step in 1604 of forbidding the practice of exorcism (known as *Canon* 72), except where the bishop gave license. Notably, no such licenses to practice exorcism were ever issued.[80] The belief and practice of cessationism had now become firmly established within mainstream Protestantism throughout Europe.

PASTOR KEN DISCOVERS EMPOWERMENT

Something deep within my spirit has always known that Jesus longed to bring greater levels of healing and freedom to me. However, my faith journey took me on a path where much of my training minimized this part of Jesus's ministry. As a result, Jesus has had to do much re-training of me over the last number of years.

Although I would have never said this (for I knew there was One God, existing eternally in three persons), functionally in my early years of faith, I journeyed with God as though the Trinity was Father, Son, and Holy Bible.

---

78   Shaw, *Miracles in Enlightenment England*, 27-8.

79   Keener, *Miracles: The Credibility of the New Testament Accounts,* 280.

80   Shaw, *Miracles in Enlightenment England*, 28.

What I mean by this is that scripture was the only voice I allowed God to speak within my life. OH, THE IRONY!!! Jesus himself said he would speak and that his sheep would know his voice! Ha! What fun Jesus has had with me as he re-trains me in his good and kind ways.

Because of my training and background that dispelled the voice of the Holy Spirit, I could not simply "trust my gut" or other's experience when it came to healing and deliverance. I had to first see this need in the scriptures and then experience it firsthand. At the beginning of my journey, Jesus first took me to Luke 4/Isaiah 61, where his mission is summed up as one of preaching, healing, and delivering (again, the humor and regret that all my training was only in the first of these three).

Jesus had me meditate in this passage for an entire summer. During that time, I found myself camping with some close friends. Late one evening, as my wife and I sat by the fire while our kids slept, we heard death-like shrills coming from a short distance away. As I heard them, I immediately jumped up and began to run toward the shrills. My wife called out, "what are you going to do?" I called back, "no idea, so say a prayer." As I got to the origin of the sound of the shrills, there was a man who was both high and demonically manifesting in a way I had never seen. With relatively little success, two large men were trying to hold him back from a woman he was trying to harm. I ran up to him; I did not touch him, looked him in the eyes, and said nothing… that's right… NOTHING! I did not yet have any words or had received training on "how to" handle demonic manifestations at this stage in my journey. The moment we locked eyes, BOOM, he collapsed straight to the ground, completely limp.

I was shocked! I said nothing to the people there! I immediately walked away, completely stunned! All I did was show up, and from there, Jesus took over. The entire next day, people from the campground approached my friends and me, asking, "who are you" or "how'd you do that." To which I simply said, "Not sure, but I know it has something to do with Jesus inside me, and I need to figure that out."

Figuring it out is precisely what I have been doing since then. I still have much to learn on this side of heaven. However, since then, Jesus has consistently brought scriptures to me, then brought them to life in my experience. I know Jesus will be good and kind to you in your journey as well. I trust that he will use this book to help train you to be a part of the ministry of bringing healing and freedom to others in his name.

THE AGE OF ENLIGHTENMENT

The Age of Enlightenment (approximately 1600-1800) is thought to have built upon the thinking of fourth-century BCE philosopher Hippocrates. He was the pioneer who championed looking for natural causes for disease rather than spiritual causes.[81] It wouldn't be until the seventeenth century when this idea was further developed and popularized by people such as Benedict Spinoza in 1670 and Scottish philosopher David Hume in 1730.[82] Hume promoted the idea that what is true can be objectively measured and observed, exclusively from a scientific perspective, rather than trusting in the belief of supernatural phenomena.[83]

As an illustration of the growing disparagement from the academic elite towards those holding a spiritual worldview, Twelftree quotes Hume in his work, *On Human Nature,* where he states that miracles "…are observed chiefly to abound among ignorant and barbarous nations…."[84] There was an enormous impact upon society as a result of this philosophy. In the words of Craig Van Gelder,

---

[81]   Kee, *Medicine, Miracle, Magic,* 30.

[82]   Neill K. Foster, *Sorting out the Supernatural* (Camp Hill, Pennsylvania: Christian Publications, 2001), 2.

[83]   Keener, *Miracles: The Credibility of the New Testament Accounts,* 114.

[84]   Twelftree, *In the Name of Jesus,* 136.

The rational construction of reality gave rise to a very distinct cultural perspective known as the Enlightenment worldview. Its distinct beliefs and values were foundational for the emergence of what we have come to know as modern Western culture... Objective science, with its practice of disciplined observation and the logical use of reasons, was accepted as the preferred method for developing knowledge, and in this knowledge a dichotomy was established between facts and values. Facts were identified as true and reliable knowledge produced by rational, scientific thought; values were relegated to the arena of personal and private choice.[85]

The science of mental illness further developed and identified physiological conditions formerly attributed to demonic influence.[86] What couldn't be observed empirically was discarded by the intellectual class. Belief in the supernatural became marginalized in the public eye. From the perspective of Protestants, this posed both a benefit and a challenge. On the one hand, disbelief in the supernatural played well into their criticism of the Catholic Church. It helped them place scripture as the ultimate authority over and above the need for the intermediary role of the 'wonderworker' priest.

On the other hand, the scientific worldview posed a challenge to religious belief of any kind, which fostered the idea of deism[87]

---

[85] Craig Van Gelder, "Mission in the Emerging Postmodern Condition." *The Church Between Gospel & Culture: The Emerging Mission in North America* (Grand Rapids, Michigan: William B. Eerdmans Publishing, 1996), 117.

[86] Daunton-Fear, *Healing in the Early Church,* 163.

[87] Definition of "deism" from, George Thomas Kurian, ed. *Nelson's Dictionary of Christianity*. (Nashville: Thomas Nelson, 2005), Pg. 210. - "An often anti-Christian philosophy substituting natural religion for revealed religion and disbelieving all miracles and supernatural events in the Bible. Deists believe that God created the world but does not actively participate in its running or in human affairs and is simply irrelevant."

within the Church. However, this isn't to suggest that belief in demons and the practice of exorcism and healing ceased during the age of the Enlightenment. Indeed, this was essentially the case among intellectuals.

However, among the masses across Europe, there remained great diversity of thought and practice concerning the miraculous.[88] Such dichotomy between these worldviews, a separation between the viewpoints of the elite, intellectual class and the general populations, seems to be a predictable phenomenon throughout cultures and over millennia.

From the time of Constantine in the fourth century to the height of the Enlightenment in the seventeenth century, healing and deliverance receded dramatically in the Church. Where scantly present, it was most frequently expressed in rote ritual or masquerading in pagan rites and superstition. In short, it bore no resemblance to the model of Jesus that he passed on, that which was further demonstrated in the first 250 years of the Church.

Failing to see both healing and deliverance as critical facets to the disciple-making process and essential vehicles in evangelistic endeavor, the Church predictably lacked a compelling reality to an increasingly skeptical world. As a result, what little remained in the realm of Christian faith was disproportionally cognitive-only. And yet, these fourteen hundred dark years were soon to be again reignited by the persistent and indefatigable light of Jesus Christ.

---

[88]   Shaw, *Miracles in Enlightenment England*, 181.

CHAPTER EIGHT

RE-ASCENT OF HEALING AND DELIVERANCE

The light shines in the darkness,
and the darkness has not overcome it.

—John 1:5

Most cultural and sociological phenomena are, to some degree, cyclical. Pendulums swing. Tides recede and return. The Sun sets and then rises again. Such was the case with the ministries of healing and deliverance in the church. At the height of the heady days of The Enlightenment emerged a deep hunger for something more than a cognitive faith within Western Christianity. Increasingly, people were interested in authentic, divine experience. This pendulum, between intellectual and experiential faith, predictably swings throughout history, and I hope that the church today can find her way to fully embrace both. The power of Christ is intended to be made manifest in both integrated arenas.

JOHN WESLEY

By the mid-seventeenth century, exorcism among Protestants was either banned altogether or relegated to mere symbolic gesture within infant baptism rituals.[89] Although small demonstrations of healing and exorcism had popped up from time to time, none proved to have any lasting impact until the arrival of John Wesley in eighteenth-century England. Wesley held a deep interest in the ministry of the Holy Spirit and the subsequent experiential nature of the believer's relationship with God. This provided space for the spiritual to impact the physical and observable world through healing and exorcism, among other things.[90] Wesley looked more so to the experiential faith of the early church fathers rather than the intellectual faith of Augustine (as Luther and Calvin had done). Thus, Wesley and his Methodist followers had less of an intellectual view of spiritual matters, and they appreciated the necessity of both orthodox belief and personal experience of God.[91] Wesleyan scholar Robert Webster contends,

> If there was anything that set the Methodists at odds with the dominant trends of the Enlightenment, however, it was their commitment to a belief in the existence of an invisible world. For John Wesley, and many of his followers in the eighteenth century, the belief in the existence of the supernatural was a fabric of their religious consciousness that they refused to dismiss."[92]

Despite criticism and even mockery from others for holding such a view, Wesley was neither apologetic nor ashamed of his stance on the supernatural. He was challenged both by secular Enlightenment thinkers as well as people of faith arguing for

---

[89]   Nischan, "The Exorcism Controversy and Baptism in the Late Reformation," 46.

[90]   Porterfield, *Healing in the History of Christianity*, 165-7.

[91]   Ben Witherington, *The Problem with Evangelical Theology: Testing the Exegetical Foundations of Calvinism, Dispensationalism and Wesleyanism* (Waco: Baylor University Press, 2005), 172, 181.

[92]   Webster, *Methodism and the Miraculous*, 9.

cessationism. His conviction was in an active, supernatural God as part of the core identity of the people of God.[93]

As a leader living within the Enlightenment period and the rise of scientific theory, Wesley didn't appeal to blind belief. Instead, he encouraged careful thought and consideration of the sciences, including that of medical advancements.[94] Wesley took something of a scientific approach to the miraculous, insisting upon reliable evidence for healing. He encouraged the scientific method in the discovery of faith and practice about the miraculous.[95] It is likely this balanced approach, embracing both science and the supernatural, helped give the Methodist movement some legs to run on.

Wesley practiced not only divine healing but exorcism as well. Collins states that "Wesley himself believed in the power of witchcraft, demon possession and frequently practiced exorcism himself; moreover, he used this belief to refute 'skeptics denying supernatural intervention in the world.'"[96]

In many respects, Wesley came upon the demonic and exorcism by sheer accident. In 1739, he stumbled upon several dramatic demonic manifestations, which led him to eventually discover that demons could be controlled on command, "In the name of Jesus."

By the latter eighteenth century, exorcism was part of the ongoing ministry of Methodists.[97] In Wesley's personal journals, over sixty miracles are recorded between 1739 and 1742, followed by approximately ten per year in the 1750s.[98] Daniel R. Jennings, in his work, *The Supernatural Occurrences of John Wesley*, compiled categories of miracles from *The Works of John Wesley*, citing no less than

---

93 Webster, *Methodism and the Miraculous*, 10-11, 33, 72.

94 Ibid., 31, 167.

95 Shaw, *Miracles in Enlightenment England*, 178-9.

96 James M. Collins, *Exorcism and Deliverance Ministry in the Twentieth Century* (Eugene, Oregon: Wipf and Stock, 2009), 140.

97 Webster, *Methodism and the Miraculous*, 77-80.

98 Shaw, *Miracles in Enlightenment England*, 178.

twenty-three stories explicitly related to exorcism and demonic activity.[99] Wesley didn't search out demonic activity but instead began to recognize it, and he grew to bring freedom to captive people better.[100] On numerous counts, we can see the proliferation of healing and deliverance under Wesley as he aligned the practices of these with the model of Jesus. Methodism remains one of the most prolific disciple-making movements within Christian history. One can't miss the deep connection between its success and its full embrace of the supernatural.

With pivotal individuals such as John Wesley, the Age of the Enlightenment provided sweeping changes and broadening views in the modern world. Worldviews with perspectives about God and the supernatural diversified to include skeptics, atheists, deists, and those who held to supernatural beliefs. [101]As Shaw states, "The essential point about mid-eighteenth-century Britain is that a range of ideas and opinions on the miraculous and the wondrous, the ordinary and the extraordinary existed."[102] Miraculous occurrences were reported from various streams of the church during this period: Anabaptists, Quakers, Pietists, and Moravians. Curiously, yet predictably, in times of history when the cultural elites despise supernatural activity, it is only later discovered that they fail to represent more widespread belief, and they are also frequently in opposition to the quiet-majority mainstream.

It was Wesley, however, that set the stage for the church to move beyond the sporadic demonstration of the miraculous and

---

[99] Jennings also relates a broader variety of supernatural occurrences within Wesley's ministry: healing (including healing of cancer, blindness, a cripple, 'slain in the Spirit,' holy laughter, tongues, trances, prophecy, angelic appearances, dreams and visions.

[100] Jennings, Daniel R., *The Supernatural Occurrences of John Wesley* (Self-Published, Sean Multimedia, 2012).

[101] Keener, *Miracles: The Credibility of the New Testament Accounts,* 380.

[102] Shaw, *Miracles in Enlightenment England,* 177.

towards its centrality in practice. Those who followed in his footsteps could also develop the experiential nature of faith, with space for healing and exorcism, because of his interest in the Holy Spirit. In fact, most twentieth-century expressions of healing and exorcism in the Western church can be traced back to the Holiness branch of the Methodist movement, founded by Wesley, including the eventual birthing of the Pentecostal movement.[103]

NINETEENTH CENTURY

As we continue to trace the development of exorcism and deliverance in what has become the Western evangelical church, we must focus almost exclusively upon the Holiness branch of Methodism and, in particular, its pursuit of divine healing.[104] Nineteenth-century pioneers further developed theology and practice within divine healing (and occasional exorcisms), such as Johann Christoph Blumhardt (1805-1880) and Dorothea Trudel (1813-62). These individuals did much to inspire others who would spawn movements and subsequent denominations.[105]

Among evangelicals in the nineteenth century, there was an impetus surrounding the completion of the Great Commission. In the wake of Methodism's experiential nature, this urgency spawned a newfound desire to see the power of the Holy Spirit returned to the church. Openness and expectancy were on the rise for divine

---

[103]   Porterfield, *Healing in the History of Christianity,* 168.

[104]   It should be noted that exorcisms and healings continued to be experienced and developed within the Catholic Church during these centuries, however such reference is beyond the scope of this study.

[105]   Keener, *Miracles: The Credibility of the New Testament Accounts,* 387-390.

healings, exorcism, and the reception of unknown tongues in the context of missions.[106]

CHRISTIAN AND MISSIONARY ALLIANCE INFLUENCE

Most development in the West related to deliverance and healing in the twentieth and twenty-first centuries can be traced back to the Welsh Revival of 1904-05 and the subsequent launching of the Pentecostal-movement in the Azusa Street Revival of 1906.

Reaching even further back, other movements also experiences divine, supernatural manifestations. One such movement is the Christian and Missionary Alliance (CMA). With its globally-distributed periodical, it is believed to have been instrumental in the advance of the Pentecostal movement, including the eventual spreading of ideas related to the supernatural.[107] That said, and because the CMA is the denominational background of this author, let's take a brief dive into the emergence of deliverance and exorcism within the CMA context.

Along with other streams of the holiness movement, the Christian and Missionary Alliance and its founder, A.B. Simpson, were highly pursuant of experientially rediscovering the person of Jesus and the power of the Holy Spirit. This led to the rediscovery of the spiritual authority that the believer has in Christ; the authority to overcome the enemy's schemes, including those related to sin and sickness.[108]

---

[106] Gary B. McGee, "The Radical Strategy on Modern Mission: Linkage of Paranormal Phenomena with Evangelism," *The Holy Spirit and Mission Dynamics, Evangelical Missiological Society Series,* number 5, (Pasadena: William Carey Library, 1997), 94.

[107] Donald E. Miller, Kimon H Sargeant, Richard Flory, eds. *Spirit and Power: The Growth and Global Impact of Pentecostalism* (New York, Oxford Press, 2013), 21.

[108] Paul L. King, *Genuine Gold: The Cautiously Charismatic Story of the Early Christian and Missionary Alliance,* (Tulsa, Oklahoma: Word & Spirit Press, 2006), 27-29.

This combination of the pursuit of divine healing and the authority of the believer set the stage for the ministry of deliverance to become inevitable, especially in the context of expanding global mission. Simpson related sickness to the work of Satan, either directly or indirectly.[109] Some historians cite Simpson and other Holiness movement leaders as those who normalized divine healing in nineteenth and early twentieth-century America.[110] As noted in Simpson's own words in his 1882 periodical,

> ... how intimately the Scriptures associate disease with sin and death as evils alike originating from Satan and second, as alike remedied by the manifestation of the Son of God in his finished work.[111]

Simpson believed that the believer in Christ has access to the victory of Jesus to overthrow every aspect of Satan's power. While the ministry of healing in the early days of the CMA is well known, less familiar is its experience in the ministry of deliverance. Later in that same year, 1882, Simpson argued specifically for the ministry of deliverance, "Christ still casts out devils, and his people should claim his unchanged power for the wretched victims of Satan whom God brings us."[112] Perhaps surprising to some today, the ministry of deliverance is nothing new to the Christian and Missionary Alliance.

---

[109] Bernie A. Van De Walle, *The Heart of the Gospel: A.B. Simpson, the Fourfold Gospel, and Late Nineteenth-Century Evangelical Theology* (Eugene, Oregon: Wipf and Stock, 2009), 129.

[110] Keener, *Miracles: The Credibility of the New Testament Accounts,* 386-90.

[111] A.B. Simpson, "The Doctrinal Ground of Prayer for the Sick", *The Word, the Work and the World,* vol. 1, no. 1 (January 1882), 17.

[112] A. B. Simpson, "Power over Evil Spirits", *The Word, the Work and the World,* vol. 1, no. 3 (March 1882), 105.

Such early beliefs within the CMA eventually became practice. An 1887 article in the same periodical tells of an exorcism within the context of missions in China.[113] Another time, in 1890, one of the first vice presidents of the CMA, Dr. George Peck, was afflicted by demonic forces characterized by pneumonia and demonic manifestations. His colleague, C.W. Morehouse, prayed for healing and cast out the demons. The experience quickly launched Peck into a ministry of healing and deliverance that reached national stature. In 1895, at a CMA convention at Old Orchard, Maine, Peck spoke on casting out demons. These developments emerged within the early CMA, fortunately, without an obsessive fixation on the ministry of exorcism and deliverance.[114] Their passion, rightly so, was upon Christ himself.

The Holiness movement of the nineteenth century never saw deliverance as primary to its ministry; it remained somewhat peripheral. However, their theological development embraced an unseen, spiritual realm along with an understanding of the authority of Christ in the believer, and this provided the framework for the recovery and the rapid expansion of deliverance ministry in the twentieth century, which we will explore in the next chapter.[115] Such a foundation was needed to rescue these foundational Kingdom ministries of Jesus from sixteen centuries of decline, neglect, and dormancy.

A DREAM LEADS SCOTT TO DELIVERANCE MINISTRY

It all started with a dream. I was in a dark apartment I didn't recognize, along with two other people. I was going from room to room, touching

---

113   King, *Genuine Gold,* 28.

114   Ibid., 28-29.

115   Collins, *Exorcism and Deliverance Ministry in the Twentieth Century,* 12.

random objects and praying. Each time I prayed, a small, black swirl-shaped apparition would appear, no bigger than the palm of my hand. As I prayed, these swirls would shoot out of the apartment like a shooting star. That was the dream... weird, I know! I very rarely remember my dreams—I sleep like a hibernating bear most nights! So when I do remember a dream, I pray about it, asking Jesus if there is something he is trying to tell me or show me.

I had just started a sabbatical at my church (literally day three!). Awaking from the dream, I got up and sat at the small white desk near my bed and began to pray and write down the dream. I felt Holy Spirit whisper to me: "I am calling you into something new. I am expanding your ministry and answering your prayer to have more impact for the kingdom." That sounded awesome! But before I could finish praying and writing, my cell phone rang. I was tempted to leave it—after all, I was on sabbatical! But I checked to see if it might be a friend or my mother calling (honest ...!), only to see that it was a man who was loosely connected to the church where I pastor. He would have no idea I was on a leave from ministry, so I answered the call, intending to direct him to anyone else but myself... but I soon learned this wouldn't be possible, and it was not what the Lord had in mind.

This was a divine appointment! I had no previous experience with deliverance—I thought that was for "special" Christian leaders, and mostly in faraway places. This day, I would wake up to a new purpose! This man gave me the address of a mother and adult son who lived together. They were having a very rough time—addiction to alcohol and prescription drugs, domestic issues, etc. As I visited with the mom, it was clear that she was drunk, but there was more to it than that—she moaned, wailed, and had sudden outbursts of profane anger. My spiritual alarm bells were going off, and with no training or knowledge to draw on, I did the only thing I could do—follow the prompting of Holy Spirit.

I looked at this woman and called forth any evil that was inside this woman. After a bumbling time of commanding this evil spirit to stop harming this woman, the spirit moaned and said: "what do you want with me?" What was not so obvious before became crystal clear. I wanted the demon to

leave and leave her alone! So, I simply said, "leave now in Jesus's name!"
The woman slumped back into her couch and promptly fell asleep for an hour
while I talked to the son. Later, the dream from the night before made sense.
It is no coincidence that one week later, I would attend an event that would
help train me in the practice of deliverance. I didn't know it at the time, but
God is funny that way! Since going through a very carefully crafted process of
training, I have helped many, many people find freedom from the torment of
evil spirits and greater freedom in Christ. I have also since helped train others
to do the same. The impact on my church community, and well beyond, has
been both humbling and exciting to see!

MODERN WORLDVIEW

As already demonstrated, the Age of Enlightenment did much to
alter the Western worldview, including that of the church. The matter of worldview has tremendous implications as to whether or not a
local church, or the global church, will embrace the biblical and historical practices of healing and deliverance. Fuller Seminary professor Charles Kraft has stated that the church's biggest problem today
is the "secularization of Christianity." Whereas the church's posture
is meant to be supernatural, today most of the answers the church
has are "secular, from the world of psychology, self-help and leadership best practices."[116] A colleague of Kraft, Paul Hiebert, describes
the implications this worldview shift has had upon the church,

> Another consequence was to divide the world into nat-
> ural and supernatural realms. The former is the domain
> of science and deals with material realities as if they are
> mechanistically determined. The latter is the domain of

---

[116] Charles H. Kraft, interview by author, South Pasadena, California, February 19,
2018.

religion and deals with spirits, miracles, feelings and values. The effect of this metaphor on Christianity in the West has been devastating. Christianity has been privatized, relegated to personal piety, while science controls public truth and life. Within Christianity, it has led to a division between evangelism and social concern.[117]

Oz Guinness, in *Impossible People,* argues that the church resides in a surrounding worldview that not only accepts the reality of spiritual entities—it also can't tolerate them. To tolerate them would necessitate the recognition of an authority which would need to be submitted to. Of this conflict, he states,

> ... in our world in which 'everyone is now everywhere,' there are no deeper clashes than the conflicts between religions and ideologies, and at their depth or height such clashes are rooted in conflicts that go beyond the purely natural, secular or even human. Seen properly, such conflicts are supernatural and even demonic....[118]

This worldview has poured into the church in recent decades with devastating results, effectively hamstringing her ability to respond to the spiritual realities and battles of the day. Gratefully, as the twentieth century progressed, so did the emergence of balanced and rooted approaches to incorporate healing and deliverance as critical facets of the disciple-making process.

---

[117] Paul G. Hiebert, "The Gospel in Our Culture: Methods of Social and Cultural Analysis." *The Church Between Gospel & Culture: The Emerging Mission in North America* (Grand Rapids, Michigan: William B. Eerdmans Publishing, 1996),146-7.

[118] Oz Guinness, *Impossible People: Christian Courage and the Struggle for the Soul of Civilization* (Downers Grove, Ill: IVP Press, 2016), Kindle edition, chapter 3, location 1178.

CHAPTER NINE

TWENTIETH CENTURY STREAMS

Perhaps Satan's best deception is its general success
in concealing its own reality from the human mind. [119]
                    —Scott Peck, psychiatrist and author

The nineteenth century saw sporadic forward movement on the practice of healing and deliverance. In contrast, the twentieth century saw a reawakening of these biblical and historical ministries. To better understand the various ways healing and deliverance developed in the twentieth century, James M. Collins provides a helpful framework. [120] Collins notes four primary streams of twentieth-century deliverance and exorcism: Charismatic-Pentecostal, Evangelical Fundamentalist, Enthusiastic Sacramental (i.e., Catholic), and Late Twentieth Century Convergence.

A brief review of each stream follows, identifying the primary literature and leaders within these respective movements, along with their contributions to the larger conversation, theology, and practice of deliverance and healing. Admittedly, the focus of the

---

[119]   Peck, Scott M. *People of the Lie: The Hope for Healing Human Evil* (New York, Simon and Schuster, 1983), 208.

[120]   James M. Collins, *Exorcism and Deliverance Ministry in the Twentieth Century* (Eugene, Oregon: Wipf and Stock, 2009).

following pages is more towards deliverance than healing. At the end of this chapter, I will illustrate how these various forms are significantly collapsing into a more unified and robust approach that is demonstrating broader appeal in the Western church. Most Christian readers will be able to locate their own church experience in one (or more) of these four streams.

CHARISMATIC PENTECOSTAL DELIVERANCE

Building off the dualist theological perspective (recognizing a dark, spiritual realm that is combatant towards the church) and practical foundations from the Holiness movement, early Pentecostals embraced healing and deliverance ministries. The Azusa Street revival that began in Los Angeles on April 9, 1906, did little to innovate their thinking and practice. Deliverance was already pre-existing to early Pentecostalism through eccentric figures such as John Alexander Dowie (1847-1907) of Zion City, Illinois.[121]

Post-Azusa Street, the practice of deliverance didn't spread among individuals; it remained significantly an itinerant ministry associated with high-profile faith healers, especially in the 1940s and 1950s. Regrettably, this didn't result in the equipping of the broader church towards a shared ministry.[122] In his publication, *God's Generals,* Roberts Liardon notes and illustrates how many of these high-powered itinerants had unfortunate and regretful endings to their ministries.[123] This is a warning to the church today: supernatural ministry sequestered to specialists rarely turns out well, especially when primarily displayed on auditorium stages. Jesus's ministries of healing and deliverance were always meant to be

---

[121]   Collins, *Exorcism and Deliverance Ministry in the Twentieth Century,* 17-20.

[122]   Collins, *Exorcism and Deliverance Ministry in the Twentieth Century,* 37.

[123]   Liardon, Roberts, *God's Generals: Why They Succeeded and Why Some Failed* (New Kensington, PA: Whitaker House, 1996) and *God's Generals: The Healing Evangelists* (New Kensington, PA: Whitaker House, 2011).

highly personal and in a wide scope of settings outside of religious gatherings. This ministry was to be carried out by the church at large, wherever Christ-followers found themselves, and in every facet of society.

Deliverance ministry in early Pentecostalism was also limited in scope. Early Pentecostal theology had little room to entertain the notion that Spirit-filled, tongues-speaking believers could have any personal need for deliverance from attached, evil spirits.[124] As such, they lacked the perspective that believers could be demonized.

Expressions of deliverance within the Charismatic-Pentecostal stream saw little development until Frank and Ida Mae Hammond's book, *Pigs in the Parlor*,[125] was published in 1973. Although the Hammonds were influenced by some of the earlier teachings of Derek Prince, it was this book that found broad appeal in the heady days of renewal and revival of the early 1970s.[126] This was one of the earliest and most influential resources that provided the rationale and step-by-step instruction for deliverance ministry accessible to any Christian, not only itinerant preachers.

This stream, Charismatic-Pentecostal deliverance, popularized the concept of "trichotomy."[127] Trichotomists believe, from 1 Thessalonians 5:23, that Christ-followers consist of body, soul, and spirit, yet demons only have potential access to the body and soul. The regenerated spirit is protected in Christ; the enemy can't touch it.[128] This development was a significant contribution. This belief allowed the ministry of deliverance to be seen as a normal,

---

[124] Collins, *Exorcism and Deliverance Ministry in the Twentieth Century*, 22.

[125] Hammond, Frank and Ida Mae, *Pigs in the Parlor: A Practical Guide to Deliverance* (1973. Reprint, Kirkwood, MO: Impact Books, 2010).

[126] Collins, *Exorcism and Deliverance Ministry in the Twentieth Century*, 65.

[127] Although the Hammonds presented the concept, they didn't utilize the term, "trichotomy" in *Pigs in the Parlor*. The word has become common nomenclature to describe this concept across the various streams of deliverance.

[128] Hammond, *Pigs in the Parlor*, 153-4.

and even needed, experience for believers, further establishing it as a critical facet of disciple-making, just as it was in the early church.

From the Hammonds onward, the Charismatic-Pentecostal stream saw a proliferation of authors and leaders in the field. Derek Prince (1915-2003) was the most influential figure with numerous practical books to train and equip the church. His crucial contribution was how he normalized deliverance; he argued that many, if not most Christians, need deliverance. To neglect this need would result in the believer continuing to needlessly battle against the unseen world.[129] Prince was an early proponent of this idea:

> [Jesus] never sent anyone out to preach the Gospel without specifically instructing and equipping that person to take action against demons in the same way that He himself did. I can find no basis anywhere in the New Testament for an evangelistic ministry that does not include the expelling of demons.[130]

Former Catholic priest Francis MacNutt (1925-2020) is another key figure within the Charismatic-Pentecostal stream, from the view of published influence. As a highly educated Catholic priest, MacNutt grew in his understanding of exorcism within Catholicism until his experience of being filled with the Holy Spirit in 1967. This eventually led him towards the charismatic stream.[131] His signature work, *Deliverance from Evil Spirits*, written in 1995 and subsequently reprinted, continues to be a staple resource for many. In it, MacNutt argues for deliverance to be central to our

---

[129]   Derek Prince, *They Shall Expel Demons: What you need to know about demons—your invisible enemies* (Grand Rapids: Baker Book House, 1998), 59.

[130]   Ibid., 10.

[131]   Collins, *Exorcism and Deliverance Ministry in the Twentieth Century,* 56-58.

understanding of Jesus's ministry and the Gospel.[132] He champions the concept of team ministry and the gift of discernment of spirits as part of his methodology.

MacNutt's Catholic background shows up in his use of "sacred objects" such as oil, water, and salt as helpful aids in the deliverance experience.[133] I am especially appreciative of MacNutt's candor in his understanding of how people come to appreciate and participate in deliverance ministry, "Like all my friends who have become actively involved in casting out evil spirits, I got involved through experience, not theory."[134] Rarely are skeptics argued into appreciating ministries of healing and deliverance. First-hand observation is the primary vehicle to acceptance and participation .

EVANGELICAL-FUNDAMENTALIST DELIVERANCE

The Evangelical Fundamentalist stream of deliverance grew out of the aftermath of the Welsh Revival (1904-05). Over time, revival leader Evan Roberts and his associate, Jessie Penn-Lewis, regrettably grew uncomfortable with the many supernatural occurrences demonstrated in the revival. Consequently, they began to attribute these miracles as the work of demons. Because of this conviction, they drew battle lines, which culminated in Penn-Lewis's book, *War on the Saints* (1912). To be sure, the enemy can mimic supernatural occurrences. However, rather than heed the call of scripture to *"test the spirits"* (1 John 4:1) and discern good from evil, Roberts and Penn-Lewis threw out the baby with the bathwater and contended against not all, but most supernatural manifestations.

---

132   Francis MacNutt, *Deliverance from Evil Spirit: A Practical Manual* (1995. Reprint, Grand Rapids: Baker Publishing, 2009) 38.

133   MacNutt, *Deliverance from Evil Spirits,* 245f.

134   Ibid., 23.

Penn-Lewis's focal points were as follows: demons deceive, and deceived people are demonized; "tarrying" (waiting) upon the Holy Spirit opens people up to the work of demons;[135] demons counterfeit the genuine works of God; therefore, much of what was occurring in the Welsh Revival was attributed by Penn-Lewis to originating with Satan. To this day, *War on the Saints* forms the foundation of the Evangelical-Fundamentalist stream.[136]

Throughout its history, the Evangelical-Fundamentalist stream of deliverance has primarily been in reaction to and opposition of the Charismatic-Pentecostal movement and its perceived excesses. This isn't surprising when one considers its dispensational and cessationist underpinnings.[137] The movement, post-Penn-Lewis, remained largely static until the mid to late twentieth century with thought and practice leaders such as Merrill F. Unger and his book, *Demonology in the World Today* (1971); Kurt E. Koch, *Demonology Past and Present* (1973); Mark Bubeck, *Overcoming the Adversary* (1984); and C. Fred Dickason, *Demon Possession & The Christian* (1987). Much of its development ran parallel to the growth and resurgence of deliverance within the Charismatic-Pentecostal stream as a reactionary movement.

This isn't to suggest that the Evangelical-Fundamentalist stream lacks contribution to the larger conversation and practice surrounding twenty-first-century deliverance ministry. With an orientation towards the authority of the Bible and academic precision, Evangelical-Fundamentalism advanced the understanding of the Christian response to the occult and those involved in it (Koch)[138] as well as the need for believers to be vigilant in spiritual

---

135   Penn-Lewis, Jessie. *War on the Saints* (1916. Reprint, Fort Washington, Pennsylvania: Christian Literature Crusade, 1995), 68f.

136   Collins, *Exorcism and Deliverance Ministry in the Twentieth Century,* 112-115.

137   Ibid., 149.

138   Kurt E. Koch, *Demonology Past and Present: Identifying and Overcoming Demonic Strongholds* (Grand Rapids, Michigan: Kregel Publications, 1973), 53-102.

warfare (Bubeck).[139] Other main-stay American evangelical leaders helped form a spiritual worldview within their circle of influence.

In 1981, Charles Swindoll produced a booklet arguing for the existence of demons, that believers can be demonized (rather than using terms of "possession" or "oppression), and that vigilance is needed in maintaining the armor of God.[140] At his 1971 crusade in Dallas, Texas, Billy Graham preached on "The Devil and Demons." In his sermon, he made statements such as, "I believe there are real demons right now [today]," and, "All who live the Christian life will meet [the devil] every day."[141]

Nevertheless, the negativity of Penn-Lewis still rings loudly in Evangelical-Fundamentalism. Dickason is perhaps the most vocal opponent to Charismatic-Pentecostal deliverance. His firmly held arguments contain several contentions: the cessation of miraculous gifts, that tongues is frequently a demonic manifestation, and that so-called gifts of discernment and prophecy are attributed to demonic activity.[142]

Ironically, as Collins concludes, the Evangelical-Fundamentalist stream (along with its opposition to all enthusiastic expressions) has come to increasingly resemble the very stream it opposes. While at the same time arguing against the Church's involvement with the supernatural, it focuses upon the supernatural manifestations of the enemy and, by extension, the same from God. Collins predicts that the Evangelical-Fundamentalist stream will eventually collapse under its inherent inconsistencies in the face of the more

---

139   Mark I. Bubeck, *Overcoming the Adversary: Warfare Praying Against the Demon* Activity (Chicago: Moody Press, 1984).

140   Charles R. Swindoll, *Demonism: How to Win Against the Devil* (Portland: Multnomah Press, 1981).

141   Our Only Hope. "Billy Graham—The Devil and Demons—Dallas TX 1971." YouTube video, 25:50. Posted September 7, 2016. https://youtu.be/lA5KUfzkfYE.

142   C. Fred Dickason, *Demon Possession & the Christian* (Chicago: Moody Press, 1987), 143.

recent stream, the Third-Wave Movement or, utilizing his specific terminology, Enthusiastic Convergence.[143] We are beginning to see such a move in the first decades of the twenty-first century.

ENTHUSIASTIC SACRAMENTAL EXORCISM

Enthusiastic-Sacramental exorcism is primarily rooted within Roman Catholicism. This stream had limited influence in re-establishing the ministry of deliverance in the Western protestant church. However, to better appreciate the larger picture, some observations are worthwhile. Like the other streams, the early 1970s proved to be catalytic in the modern development of Enthusiastic-Sacramental exorcism, often following the Charismatic-Pentecostal and Evangelical-Fundamental streams. Before this, exorcism within Roman Catholicism remained marginal and clandestine.[144]

Enthusiastic-Sacramental exorcism is essentially a version of the historical Catholic sacrament of exorcism. This stream was popularized by Malachi Martin, a former Jesuit priest, in his New York Times best-seller, *Hostage to the Devil* (1976), where he tells the story of five exorcisms that gripped readers in his day. Central to his paradigm is the idea that "the surest effect of possession in an individual... is the great loss in human quality, in "*humanness*"[145] (italics his). I tend to agree. Of Lucifer, he contends,

> ... the belief that he does not exist at all is an enormous advantage that he has never enjoyed to such a degree. It is the ultimate camouflage... to disbelieve is to be disarmed.

---

143 Collins, *Exorcism and Deliverance Ministry in the Twentieth Century,* 149-50.

144 Collins, *Exorcism and Deliverance Ministry in the Twentieth Century,* 151-52.

145 Malachi Martin, *Hostage to the Devil: The Possession and Exorcism of Five Americans* (1976. Reprint, San Francisco: Harper, 1992), 409.

If your will does not accept the existence of evil, you are rendered incapable of resisting evil.[146]

Martin's broad readership and compelling narratives drew the attention of many, including a nationally famous psychiatrist, M. Scott Peck. Peck's subsequent experimentation with exorcism and widely read books further popularized the belief in the devil and exorcism. Interestingly, Martin strongly argues that the Enneagram Personality Test is a tool used to demonize people and dissuade Christians from orthodox faith.[147]

Collins notes that given the historic rigidity of the Catholic Church, it has been slow to adapt to societal and practical implications regarding exorcism, perhaps lagging twenty years behind the other streams. Vatican II (1965) was reluctant to reform exorcism, but with the emergence of popular charismatic deliverance ministry, the Vatican issued a revised *Roman Ritual*[148] in 1999.[149] This prescribed ritual depends primarily upon the set of readings, prayers, and adjurations meant to bear authority against the residing demon. Exorcism, conducted by only a select few, is said to last up to days, weeks, months, or even years.[150] In contrast, other streams of deliverance utilize the authority the believer has in Christ, and it is a comparatively brief experience, lasting mere minutes to a few hours.

Practitioners of Enthusiastic-Sacramental exorcism such as Gabriele Amorth look disparagingly upon other forms. Deliverance conducted by laity is frowned upon, as this can quickly devolve into meaningless prayers and, at worst, practitioners can

---

[146] Ibid., xv.

[147] Ibid., xxi.

[148] Charles Wolffe, ed., *Rite of Exorcism: 1999 Rite in Latin and English* (Catholic Church: 2017).

[149] Collins, *Exorcism and Deliverance Ministry in the Twentieth Century,* 175.

[150] Elmo Nauman, *Exorcism Through the Ages,* 121.

inadvertently participate in witchcraft.[151] Martin warns of the perils of inexperienced people conducting exorcisms lest he "…dies, collapses, flees, is physically or emotionally battered beyond endurance—and all have happened during exorcisms."[152] Curiously though, Amorth also argues that exorcism ought to be a part of spiritual discipleship, albeit marginal.[153]

ENTHUSIASTIC-CONVERGENCE DELIVERANCE

The early 1980s saw the emergence of a movement known as "Third-wave Charismatics," distinct from earlier forms of Pentecostalism and other Charismatics. "Third-wavers" essentially grew out of evangelical circles pioneered by the likes of John Wimber. Some academics quickly attached to the movement, such as C. Peter Wagner and Charles Kraft of Fuller Seminary, who began to academically legitimize a position to become more thoughtful, theological, and biblical.[154] Wagner asserted that the casting out of demons is an identifying trait of the Third-wave. Interestingly, Wagner and Kraft had previous overseas mission experience, where notably, they credit direct contact with the demonic as helping form their spiritual worldview.

The Enthusiastic-Convergence stream has fostered a new reality in the ministries of healing and deliverance, namely the convergence of various elements from other streams. In the later twentieth century and early twenty-first century, the ministry of healing and deliverance moved away from the itinerants and towards the mobilization of the broader church. The progression of

---

151   Gabriele Amorth, *An Exorcist Tells His Story* (San Francisco: Ignatius Press, 1999), 42-3.

152   Martin, *Hostage to the Devil*, 157.

153   Amorth, *An Exorcist Tells His Story*, 112.

154   Collins, *Exorcism and Deliverance Ministry in the Twentieth Century*, 100-105.

this is easily identifiable. C. Peter Wagner and John Wimber taught their infamous classes from 1982–1985 at Fuller Seminary, Pasadena, "MC510: Signs, Wonders and Church Growth." In the words of Wimber, the course was designed to equip pastors to "do the stuff." Classroom practicums included healing the sick, operating in the prophetic, and casting out demons.[155]

Graham H. Twelftree, who currently serves as Academic Dean at the London School of Theology, emerged from the Vineyard movement of John Wimber. He is currently viewed across academia as one of the leading authorities on exorcism in antiquity and a contributor to the quest for the historical Jesus. His writings such as *Jesus the Exorcist: A Contribution to the Study of the Historical Jesus* (1992, 2010) and *In the Name of Jesus: Exorcism among Early Christians* (2007), have provided theological and historical underpinnings to the convergence stream of deliverance.

Neil T. Anderson's book *The Bondage Breaker*, first published in 1990, was widely consumed by Evangelical Christians in North America. Unlike previous Evangelical-Fundamentalist practitioners (Penn-Lewis and Unger), Anderson chose not to attack Charismatic-Pentecostal practitioners in deliverance. Instead, he focused on a "truth encounter" approach to achieving freedom.[156] Most Charismatic-Pentecostal practitioners focused on the presence of demons as the loci for change. However, Anderson, while acknowledging the presence of demons, focused on getting rid of the matters of the soul that give the enemy ground such as misbelief, bitterness, rebellion, pride, etc.[157]

---

[155]   C. Peter Wagner, *Wrestling with Alligators, Prophets and Theologians: Lessons from a Lifetime in the Church—a Memoir* (Ventura, CA: Regal, 2010), 124-130.

[156]   Collins, *Exorcism and Deliverance Ministry in the Twentieth Century,* 193-195.

[157]   Neil T. Anderson, *The Bondage Breaker* (Eugene, Oregon: Harvest House Publishers, 1990), 185ff.

Anderson explicitly states that he doesn't practice casting out demons but instead focuses on removing "ground" and replacing it with biblical truth. [158] As such, I don't consider his definition of "deliverance" to be legitimate. If truth encounters were sufficient, Jesus would have done that alone without commanding his followers to cast out demons. Interestingly, I have come across many people who have felt some relief through truth encounter approaches, only to experience more profound freedom through actual deliverance. Charles Kraft specifically challenges "truth encounter" approaches:

> There are ministries that teach that once the legal rights have been taken away, the demons go on their own. I don't trust that teaching. What seems to happen in my ministry is that even very weak demons, those from whom the things they cling to have been taken, are usually still there even after their legal right are gone.[159]

Nevertheless, Anderson's contribution to the worldview of Western evangelical believers is enormous. Anderson moved deliverance ministry away from more subjective approaches and towards truth-based approaches. His work on defeating the grounds of the enemy through truth encounters is certainly to be commended.

Anderson's writings proved to be tremendously popular with curious evangelicals and charismatics alike. Throughout his book, he presents compelling biblical evidence for the existence of demons, how they operate, and the nature of spiritual warfare. Anderson makes the bold assertion that, in his opinion, as many as eighty-five percent of believers are in some measure of spiritual bondage.[160]

---

[158]   Ibid., 208.

[159]   Charles H. Kraft, *Defeating Dark Angels: Breaking Demonic Oppression in the Believer's Life* (1992. Reprint, Grand Rapids: Baker Publishing, 2011), 247.

[160]   Anderson, *The Bondage Breaker,* 107.

Despite not advocating for verbally casting out demons, Anderson helped develop a worldview that acknowledges that evil spirits can impact the lives of Christians. He provided a framework of practice that is down-to-earth and accessible to both clergy and laity alike. Anderson lamented the loss of personal renunciation of the enemy in the life of the evangelical church, which has been retained in the rote traditions of confirmation by both Catholic and Orthodox traditions.[161] Essentially, he argued that the ministry that brings freedom to believers from demonic schemes needs to be part of our everyday disciple-making practices.

This evolving supernatural worldview, along with more rigorous support from evangelical academia, led to a proliferation of deliverance practitioners and approaches in the latter twentieth and early twenty-first centuries. C. Peter and Doris Wagner, early pioneers in this stream, published numerous books on the subject. Doris Wagner describes how her husband Peter would "come up with the theories" and then send her out into the field to see how it worked.[162] C. Peter Wagner's role as a prominent academic at Fuller Seminary helped to legitimize this early experimentation and formulation. In Doris Wagner's book published in 2000, she argues that the ministry of deliverance ought to be a facet of our tactics in evangelism whereby we welcome people in torment into a life of freedom in Christ.

> The point I wish to emphasize is that if deliverance is carried out at the time of conversion or shortly thereafter, it is my guess that it can be a great factor in evangelism

---

[161]   Ibid., 187.

[162]   Doris M. Wagner, interview by author, Argyle, Texas, February 14, 2018.

and in sustaining a revival for the vigorous growth of the church.[163]

Charles H. Kraft, now retired Professor of Anthropology and Intercultural Communication at Fuller Seminary, is also considered a thought leader in the Enthusiastic-Convergence stream of deliverance and has published numerous books on the subject: *Defeating Dark Angels: Breaking Demonic Oppression in the Believer's Life* (1992, 2011), *Two Hours to Freedom: A Simple and Effective Model for Healing and Deliverance* (2010), *Deep Wounds Deep Healing* (2010), *I Give You Authority: Practicing the Authority Jesus Gave us* (2012) and *The Evangelical's Guide to Spiritual Warfare* (2015). Kraft offers his opinion that at least two-thirds of Christians in churches are demonized, including those in church leadership. From my own experience, I have no reason to dispute this claim. He essentially argues that deliverance and inner healing ministries should be normalized.[164]

Of Kraft's many contributions, of greater significance would be his popularization of the concept of the inner healing of the soul as a vital aspect of the deliverance experience. Kraft states that "demons are of secondary focus, not primary."[165] Instead of the demonic, the focus is upon removing the attachments in our soul which give the enemy access.[166] This isn't done merely via a "truth encounter" (as popularized by Anderson) but instead through an encounter with the presence of Jesus whereby our inner world of memories and wounds are healed.[167]

---

[163]   Doris M. Wagner, *How to Cast out Demons: A Guide to the Basics* (Ventura, California: Regal Books, 2000), 44.

[164]   Kraft, *Defeating Dark Angels*, 29.

[165]   Charles H. Kraft, interview by author, South Pasadena, California, February 19, 2018.

[166]   Kraft, *Defeating Dark Angels*, 112, 258.

[167]   Charles H. Kraft, *Two Hours to Freedom: A Simple and Effective Model for Healing and Deliverance* (Grand Rapids, Michigan: Chosen Books, 2010), 63.

The writings of Third-Wave leaders, such as Wagner and Kraft, have led to a proliferation of practitioners and authors presenting various approaches. What has converged are the realms of practice, academic thoughtfulness, and missional advance pertaining to healing and deliverance. In the words of Collins,

> Subordinating deliverance ministry to the practical goal of world evangelization and the spiritual warfare necessary to achieve it proved to be a banner around which Evangelical-Fundamentalist practitioners of deliverance could join Charismatics, particularly since the boundaries between the two groups has already substantially eroded in any case.[168]

Consequentially, deliverance and healing ministries are rapidly moving away from the sphere of the clergy only, as was the case from circa 300 through 1970, and towards the laity, which is more akin to the first 250 years of the church.

---

[168]   Collins, *Exorcism and Deliverance Ministry in the Twentieth Century*, 191.

PART THREE

RESEARCH
& ONRAMPS

CHAPTER TEN

THE EVIDENCE OF RESEARCH

*I have come into the world as a light, so that no one who believes
in me should stay in darkness.*

—Jesus (John 12:46)

For those old enough to remember, the 1989 movie *Fletch*, starring Chevy Chase, did a marvelously humorous job of framing the hypocrisy and self-interest of self-proclaimed miracle workers. The miraculous has always had both its skeptics and champions. Miracles claimed by the church frequently come under a high degree of suspicion. This is understandable as the church has often done herself little favors. We can all relay stories of self-aggrandizing televangelists peddling their miraculous wares in exchange for your credit card number. Such depictions build little credibility towards acceptance and appreciation of healing and deliverance.

Might there be some research to support the credibility of these ministries? Most books on deliverance and healing contain personal narratives of transformation and freedom. While these are both interesting and compelling, there is a need to measure the efficacy of the ministry of deliverance. Numerous scholars, historians, and professionals in the world of psychiatry and psychology have called for credible social-science research to be conducted.[169] Even the global evangelical network, the Lausanne Movement, has stated this challenge, "There is an urgent need to develop criteria and methods that allow us to evaluate [deliverance ministry] in a verifiable way."[170] This is precisely what I set out to do.

THE RESEARCH PROJECT

For my doctoral dissertation, I conducted a study to measure the perceived effects of deliverance on the well-being of forty-six Christian leaders. The individuals comprised pastors, denominational leaders, international Christian workers, lay leaders, and their spouses. Using an online survey exploring ninety-eight potential effects, I sought to answer the following question: to what extent, if any, does deliverance ministry have measurable effects in the lives of Christian leaders? Can this be determined beyond anecdotal reference through credible social-science research methodology? To my knowledge, this was the first study of its kind.

What qualifies as deliverance, one might ask? For participants to be eligible for the study, they needed to have had the following as their experience:

1. Their deliverance experience had to be conducted by one of five individuals, each of whom I was familiar with in their approach. I am one of those individuals.

---

[169] A list of such appeals can be found in: Balzer, Douglas A. "The Effect of Deliverance on the Well-Being of Christian Leaders." Doctoral diss., Alliance Theological Seminary, 2018, p. 57-60.

[170] Lausanne Movement. *Deliver us from Evil—Consultation Statement*. Official records from Nairobi 2000 gathering, 22 August 2000. Accessed online July 3, 2018, https://www.lausanne.org/content/statement/deliver-us-from-evil-consultation-statement.

2. Demonic spirits were suspected by the participant and identified by the practitioner by name and/or function. Identification could be made through various approaches: direct speech from the demon, observation of what is being demonstrated/manifested, or through spiritual discernment (See Appendix A: Info-Gathering in Deliverance).

3. Any 'ground' or rights of presence the demon(s) had were removed.[171] It should be understood that a significant element to this deliverance methodology is in the spiritual formation of the soul, especially pertaining to matters of identity in Christ, repentance, unforgiveness, emotional wounds, and so forth. In all these areas (and more), the enemy can form 'ground' or legitimacy for access. Typically, most deliverances within this form of methodology have ample time spent in ministering to the individual in these matters of soul formation and not simply casting out demons. This formation is ideal to occur in the days and weeks leading up to the deliverance experience itself. However, frequently some measure of "soul work" occurs at the point of deliverance.

---

[171] The matter of "ground" (Ephesians 4:27, Greek "topos" translated as 'ground', 'opportunity' or 'foothold') usually falls into one of two categories: captive or prisoner. Jesus came to set both free (Isaiah 61:1); however, the means to their freedom is unique. Captives are held at no fault of their own, and therefore their freedom is more about the declaration of the same; the breaking of the illegitimate hold Satan has over them through the victory and authority of Christ. Examples of "ground" to be broken for captives may include: violent or sexual trauma (especially as experienced as a child), family transference (familial secrets, vows, rituals, etc.), curses. Prisoners are held due to their own sin and therefore "ground" must be broken through personal ownership and repentance. Examples of "ground" to be broken for prisoners may include: repentance, forgiveness, renouncing lies, sexual sin, anger, violence, wounds needing to be given over to the care of Jesus, breaking agreements with false beliefs, etc.

4. The demon(s) was verbally cast out with some confirmation of its departure, either through immediate perception by the participant,[172] direct testing of the spirit(s), observation of changed behavior/experience, or spiritual discernment.

5. Prayer was offered for the healing, restorative, and filling presence of Christ to be experienced by the participant. This is the "end-game" of deliverance, not merely deliverance *from* darkness, but deliverance *to* the freedom and light that Jesus brings. Jesus lights up the dark. In such times of prayer, it is common for the person to describe a tangible experience of Christ ministering to them: healing emotional wounds and memories, a sense of the deep love of the Father, sensation of warmth and/or tingling physically, experience of silence and rest in their mind/soul, a deep peace, a sense of God affirming their identity as one loved by him, etc.

6. To diminish any perceived elevation of scoring due to emotionalism of heightened subjectivity, everyone completed the survey a minimum of six months after their deliverance experience. The maximum time differential between their deliverance experience and the survey taken was four years, with the average being one to two years.

---

[172] It is not uncommon for a participant in deliverance to have a sense of demons departing, either through 'seeing' them depart in their mind's eye, a physical sensation of departure or release, or the immediate cessation of the sense of torment or negative influence brought on by the demonic entity (i.e., anxiety, depression, anger).

RESEARCH HIGHLIGHTS[173]

The survey asked participants to respond to ninety-eight questions along a continuum of five possible responses:

Significant increase
Increase
No change or Not Applicable
Decrease
Significant Decrease

REDUCED NEGATIVE REALITIES

The following percentage of Christian leaders noted a significant decrease of the following dynamics:

Reduced felt shame 83%
Reduced condemning thoughts 78%
Reduced discouragement 76%
Reduced anxiety 75%
Reduced fear of failure 72%
Reduced felt need to inflate self 72%
Reduced drive for perfectionism 69%
Reduced sense of inner turmoil & panic 67%
Reduced sense of pride and arrogance 65%
Reduced felt need to compare self to others 63%
Reduced felt need to be defensive 63%
Reduced sense of self-performance in ministry 61%
Reduced feeling of inadequacy in ministry 52%

---

[173] The constraints of this book do not allow for a full reporting of the results for the research project. One can access the larger data summary in my dissertation, linked in my website: www.dougbalzer.com. There I report and elaborate on many other themes emerging from the data.

Reduced sense of loneliness 50%

Reduced aggression toward others 49%

Reduced sense of life as frantic and chaotic 46%

Reduced difficulty entering into worship 46%

Reduced felt resistance to walking in truth 46%

Reduced view of opposite gender as sex objects 44%

Reduced difficulty sleeping 44%

Reduced need to medicate for stress 44%

Men: reduced feeling of misogyny 39%

Reduced dark, sexualized dreams 37%

Reduced pornographic viewing 37%

Reduced felt power of lust 35%

Reduced regular blasphemous thoughts 28%

Reduced terrorizing dreams at night 26%

Reduced desire to be violent towards others 22%

Reduced desire to take one's own life 17%

Reduced desire to harm self 13%

INCREASED POSITIVE REALITIES

The following percentage of Christian leaders noted a significant increase to the following dynamics:

Increased sense of emotional healing 96%

Increased feelings of internal peace 94%

Increased sense of spiritual authority in Christ 91%

Increased praying with boldness 89%

Increased security as a loved child of God 89%

Increased ability to cope with internal stress 89%

Increased "confessional" lifestyle 87%

Increased assurance that God can be trusted 87%

Increased hunger and love for God 85%

Increased sense of abiding joy 85%

Increased desire to see others know Christ 85%

Increased regular sense of God's presence 83%

Increased regular answers to prayer 83%

Increased ability to navigate conflict healthily 83%

Increased sense in the empowerment of Holy Spirit 80%

Increased seeing God move supernaturally 80%

Increased sense of love for others 80%

People have noticed a positive change in them 78%

Increased insight into God's Word by Holy Spirit 78%

Increased risk-taking for the mission of God 78%

Increased capacity to resist temptation 74%

Increased ability to recognize the voice of God 72%

Increased ability to express thoughts to others 72%

Increased emotional connection to spouse 71%

Increased engagement in spiritual disciplines 65%

Increased fruitfulness beyond church walls 65%

Increased time reading Bible 63%

Healthier relationship with their children 62%

Increase in patience towards others 61%

Increased satisfaction in sex life 47%

DEMONIC MANIFESTATIONS ARE BROAD IN EXPRESSION

These statistics are compelling, especially when one considers that
the median time of survey completion was 12–24 months post-de-
liverance experience. If the removal of demonic presence rendered
such identifiable results, one must conclude that *potential* demonic
manifestation can be reflected in the matters above. When I con-
verse with many church leaders, it appears that a general understanding of demonic manifestation is what one might expect on
the mission frontiers of pagan and animistic peoples: violence,

screaming, loss of physical control, etc. In short, things we read about with Jesus's encounter with the demonized man from the Gadarene region.[174]

The data demonstrates a much broader reality. If the removal of demon(s) results in, for example, less anxiety, fear, shame, condemnation, and depression, then we can rightly conclude that the presence of demons can be manifested in these very same emotional realities. Indeed, the data demonstrates that the presence of demons manifests across a broad range of negative effects: emotional, cognitive, physical, spiritual, etc.

In Western culture, relative to non-Western cultures, people are more cognitive and somewhat skeptical of paranormal activity. Therefore, demonic activity will generally remain congruent within cultural norms compared to animistic cultures. This will include demonic forces staying 'hidden' from view and embedding their strategy in what will not seem supernaturally unusual.[175] The accompanying anecdotal data[176] illustrates how Christian leaders assumed their negative thought patterns were 'normal,' only to see this considerably decrease or disappear altogether as an effect of deliverance:

> What I have most noticed here is how the clutter of negative voices in my mind is gone. I didn't realize it right away, however, it did not take long to realize the clutter was gone, and I was able to focus on what the actual voices in my mind were, the source. The power the negative voices had over me was clearly gone.

---

[174] Matthew 8:28.

[175] However, as noted in Chapter 3, the Western world is rapidly becoming more accepting of a spiritual worldview that embraces the paranormal.

[176] Anecdotal data of survey participants can be accessed via the full dissertaion report.

From guilt, shame, and remorse ... I have been set free to rest, be happy, and love freely.

Throughout my entire life, I would, at times, be overcome by depression. These depressive episodes have lifted since my deliverance.

Stress, fear, and anxiety have greatly decreased in my life.

The data is conclusive that demonic manifestation in the life of the Christian leaders surveyed has a broad range of effects, much of it surprising to those without even moderate experience in the ministry of deliverance. The implication of this is that years of intentional Christian discipleship and counseling, devoid of deliverance, are likely to be ineffectual where demonization is present. In contrast, a correct diagnosis of demonic infestation and the casting out of the same would be a more effective and concrete solution.

To illustrate this further, and assuming this survey is remotely representative of other Christian leaders, 76% of discouragement among current clergy (and laity) may be due to demonic schemes. In Christian disciple making, it would be wise to consider potential demonic involvement when people experience such realities. We should not jump to this conclusion, but to not have it as a possibility would be naïve.

The survey reveals that Christian leaders, as a whole, are far removed from the freedom Jesus intends for them. If this is true for Christian leaders, it isn't likely to be any less so for the broader church as well. What many might think is merely a normal yet challenging part of life may not be God's version of normal after all. These days, God is redefining the view of normal for many as he lights up their darkness. Here is one such story from a research participant.

LAURIE'S VICTORY OVER DEPRESSION AND SUICIDE

My journey to freedom began in a very dark place. Years of abuse, and a lack of understanding of my position as a child of God, had left me beaten and worn out. I had been in the valley of depression for several years. Medication and counseling didn't lift it. I thought about suicide daily. Looking back over my life, I can see that I carried suicide with me; as a 'back door' escape plan, I could pull out if needed. It almost became my safety net.

I had been a believer in Jesus for many years. However, I continually felt far from God. I had never fully grasped how to experience an authentic relationship with my Heavenly Father. It seemed that he was distant from me, as were most of my relationships. I had built up walls of protection in the form of self-protection. I had found some freedom at a Holy Spirit Encounter weekend previously. I learned that if I called out to God when thoughts of suicide came, the tormenting thoughts would become smaller and somewhat controlled. I was hesitantly hopeful that he may have more for me.

During a time of worship at a healing and deliverance conference, I began to see a small dark spot that wouldn't go away. When I asked Holy Spirit what it was, I clearly heard "depression and suicidal thoughts." I had no idea what to do with that information. When we met in our small group to pray for one another, I brought it up. The group prayed for me; however, nothing was resolved. At the end of our time, Doug & Teri were called over by my group members. They led me through breaking agreements I had made with lies about who I was and who God is. They rebuked and broke off words (curses) that had been spoken over me. Once the ground had been broken, the evil spirits were commanded to leave. I felt the heaviness of depression lift off of me, and the voice of suicide silenced. I knew depression and suicide were gone immediately.

Previously thoughts of suicide were with me constantly. Since deliverance, I have never experienced those taunting thoughts again and have been off all depression medication for several years. I am free! I walk in a close relationship with Jesus!

EMOTIONAL AND PHYSICAL HEALING

Surprising, in the data, are the experiences of healing in the lives of survey participants. Ninety-six percent indicated their experience resulted in some form of emotional healing. Forty-four percent showed that their experience resulted in physical healing, either a total or notable improvement. This is interesting as most deliverance experiences do not focus primarily on prayer for physical healing. What can be derived is that merely through the removal of demonic presence and the release of the transformational presence of Christ, physical healing can be expected in a significant number of people... 44% is no small number!

Anecdotes from participants regarding emotional healing speak to a range of positive effects: greater emotional/relational capacity, freedom from guilt, shame, depression, condemnation, etc. Some of the cited examples of physical healing include some measure of freedom from fatigue, back pain, allergies, infertility, bladder infection, migraine headaches, cancer, menstrual cramps, etc. To be sure, the participants identified the deliverance experience as the trigger point to such improvement and stated the efficacy six months to four years later.

Within these broad, positive effects, there are predictable patterns of direct benefit. For example, it's my experience that a significant number of people who experience terrorizing or highly sexualized dreams[177] were, in fact, past victims of sexual abuse or rape. People with such backgrounds are frequently demonized

---

[177] Demons that function as nocturnal, sexually harassing spirits are referred to as Incubus and Succubus spirits.

due to the trauma and experience predictable, adverse effects from the attached demons. The data of this study presents compelling evidence that freedom can be experienced by such individuals through deliverance.

Similarly, individuals who experienced verbal or violent abuse, especially in their younger years, will predictably experience higher degrees of demonization related to condemnation, anger, shame, etc. In this manner, practitioners of deliverance and those in psychology and psychiatry would do well to learn from and assist one another towards greater freedom being experienced by their clients.

GENDER DIFFERENCES

The average overall score of men and women is virtually identical; however, the top quartiles differ, with women exceeding that of men by 14%. This means that generally speaking, women experience a greater degree of perceived effect from deliverance on fewer items. Women experience heightened effects relative to men. However, men experience a broader range of perceived effects than do women. I can't explain this phenomenon as the contributing factors could be multiple, i.e., differences in emotional responses related to gender, the wording of survey questions providing differing resonance with gender, etc.

When we consider the scoring differences between women and men, common in women's scores are themes of identity, empowerment, and confidence in ministry. Seven of the top ten scored items for women are related to these themes:

I have a deep sense of empowerment by the Holy Spirit.
I pray with boldness for others.
I live with security in my identity as a loved child of God.

I have a sense of walking in Christ's spiritual authority.

I have assurance that God is good and can be trusted.

I see regular answers to prayer.

I live with expectancy of God's power in my ministry.

The data conclusively indicates an overall demonic scheme exists to keep women suppressed in kingdom and church ministry. Male church leaders would do well not to find themselves participating on the wrong side of the equation lest they find themselves in league with overt demonic activity. For men, the only two noted heightened differences relative to women's scores pertain to pornography and pride (desire to inflate oneself and over-compensate).

DELIVERANCE INCREASES MISSIONAL FRUITFULNESS

The data demonstrates that among Christian leaders, those who have experienced personal deliverance see an increase in the expressed mission of God through them. They describe growth in desire, boldness, spiritual empowerment and authority, expectancy, and risk-taking. Operating in the supernatural increases across the board.

A contemporary example of this dynamic can be found with Dr. Ajai Lall of Central India Christian Mission, who has seen 2,500 churches planted in India, mainly through conversion growth precipitated by signs and wonders such as healing and deliverance. A core criterion for church planter candidacy is that they must have a conversion story marked by such signs and wonders. Freely you have received, freely give.

I strongly contend, therefore, that if the church ignores and neglects the ministry of deliverance among its people in their disciple-making processes, and especially among its leaders, the extension of Christian mission will only be further hindered.

Conversely, facilitating the freedom that Jesus has purchased for all his daughters and sons through healing and deliverance will result in an increased impetus, motivation, and supernatural empowerment in mission.

EFFECTS OF DELIVERANCE INCREASES OVER TIME

A dramatic surprise emerging from the data was that the perceived effects of deliverance *increased* over time. The measured impact grew between 6–12 months-since-deliverance and 24+ months-since-deliverance by 35% on average. This depicts a significant increase in positive results over time. Such data refutes the assumption that the perception of the effects of deliverance is derived mainly from the enthusiasm of the event itself. The data suggests that the opposite is true: the further one gets away from their deliverance experience chronologically, the greater their positive related experience.

A similar dynamic is seen in the field of physiology. A child who ceases to grow physically, according to expected norms, is deemed to have something wrong. Once the ailment is eliminated, normal growth occurs on its own and without undue additional effort. The data of this project presents a similar dynamic in spiritual growth and maturity. Where a person has demonic attachments, their growth is predictably stunted. Once it has been removed, normal Christian maturity is enabled to naturally continue. This positive effect is not static but has an increasing and exponential impact as the participants' freedom takes deeper roots and finds a broader expression in their lives. Therefore, my firm conclusion from the data is that deliverance needs to play a critical role in the disciple-making process of every believer and as early as possible. Indeed, this was the case for the first 250 years of the church. Might we reclaim it in our day?

FREE INDEED!

I was somewhat stunned to see precise data refuting one of my core assumptions. Namely, that ongoing freedom gained through deliverance is highly dependent upon intentional maintenance through spiritual disciplines. The data supports the opposite position. Those who indicated no intentionality scored 130% higher on average than those who indicated moderate intention. This data represents a marked difference.

Upon reflection, I have noted many people who had gone through deliverance who described some negative areas addressed as completely resolved. With that and the current data in view, I conclude that for many areas where the achievement of freedom is realized, little to no personal intention towards maintenance is needed. Certainly this dynamic will not be relevant to all, however, in these cases, freedom is often total and complete.

This isn't to suggest further maturation isn't required, as it always is. Only that the sense of bondage is utterly gone. Further, in a minority of cases, additional intentional maintenance of freedom is needed. Indeed, for some, the ongoing assistance of a psychologist or other trained professional is critical. However, the participant in deliverance still needs to be taught how to maintain their freedom, live out new patterns, and not assume otherwise.

Interestingly, the category that received the highest positive scoring was about one's relationship with God, containing elements that describe increased intimacy with Jesus. Suppose the surveyed group is even remotely representative of broader populations of Christ-followers in the West. In that case, the good news is that the gospel we profess is far better, in effect, than our collective experience has been to date.

I must admit my initial amazement upon reflection of the data and the broad scope of impact of deliverance. Seemingly every facet of life could be impacted positively. Upon further reflection, this aligns with a biblical view that the enemy attempts to steal, kill, and destroy all that is good.[178] Conversely, where the presence of Jesus is invited and his truth is appropriated, greater freedom is a direct outcome.[179] Simply put, no area of a person's life could potentially be unaffected by the removal of demonic forces (should they be present) by the increased presence and lordship of Jesus Christ. Jesus lights up the dark.

---

[178]   John 10:10.

[179]   Luke 4:16-20.

CHAPTER ELEVEN

A SHIFT IN WORLDVIEW

For he has rescued us from the dominion of darkness and brought us into the kingdom of the Son he loves, in whom we have redemption, the forgiveness of sins.

—Colossians 1:13-14

Abraham planted a tree, a Tamarisk tree, in the desert of Beersheba. I have been to Beersheba and can assure you nothing grows quickly or easily without modern watering systems. Tamarisks survive in the desert partially because they have very deep taproots, enabling them to source water far beneath the surface. They can also thrive in the otherwise hostile salty soil conditions. Abraham planted the tree not for himself but for future generations. He knew that one day, many years later, others would be able to enjoy a respite from the hot sun in its shade. He also knew that people he'd never meet would enjoy the benefits.

The Tamarisk provides a good picture of what is needed in the Church about healing and deliverance. We're fighting an uphill battle in many ways, pushing back the fear, ignorance, deception, and neglect of 1,700 years. This is no small task. Large-scale change will seem slow at times. And yet, we don't commit to returning to orthodox faith and practice merely for ourselves. We do it for future generations.

I am frequently asked if I get frustrated with the seemingly slow pace of this shift towards a holistic gospel that embraces the supernatural. The answer is no, I do not. I have a thirty-year window in view. I believe it may take several generations to see this shift take deep root, although many bright spots can already be seen. Yet I dream of a day when children to Christ-following parents grow up with a new worldview, one where it is entirely normal to see Christ as victor over darkness and illness; and not merely metaphorical. I dream of a day when deliverance, physical, and inner healing are standard facets of disciple-making and early in the process. I dream of a day when Christ-followers are led by the Spirit to demonstrate both the spoken and demonstrated gospel with the power and presence of Jesus to those who do not yet know him.

Abraham didn't just plant a Tamarisk tree. He also received a distinct calling from God in Genesis 12:2–3.

I will make you into a great nation, and I will bless you; I will make your name great, and you will be a blessing. I will bless those who bless you, and whoever curses you I will curse; and all peoples on earth will be blessed through you.

This calling was ultimately fulfilled in the person of Jesus Christ and then passed on to each of his followers to advance in the world. What could be better news than to live under the blessing of God and extend the same blessing to others? I dream of a day when Christ-followers everywhere feel naturally empowered to give away the authority over darkness that Jesus has placed in them, bringing his supernatural restoration and blessing to others.

To better move in this direction, what follows are my recommendations to Christ-followers for planting tamarisk trees.

NEEDED: A BEHAVIORAL SHIFT IN WORLDVIEW

The Church must teach and model a biblically rooted and historically accurate worldview pertaining to the supernatural. We must throw off the shackles of myopic secularism, biblically bankrupt cessationism, social accommodation, and fear of the unfamiliar. At the core of this needed shift is recognizing the holistic nature of the gospel of Jesus Christ. A gospel that is good news not only pertaining to our eternal dwelling place, but that has broad impact in the here and now of our lives, body, soul, and spirit. The broken world around us needs us to make this shift. Can anything short of God's divine empowerment bring the redemption and blessing for which we all long?

The champions of these shifts must include all Christ-followers regardless of where their sphere of influence lies, in their homes, neighborhoods, schools, churches, marketplaces, denominations, and academic institutions. They must tell both ancient and recent stories of Jesus's transforming power. They must dive into a personal experience of the transforming Christ. They must teach not only a cognitive gospel but lead people into experiential encounters with the living Christ.

As I noted earlier, Charles Kraft observes that the Church needs to be rescued from the "secularization of Christianity," where most answers from the Church to the surrounding world have become increasingly secular-only, from the world of psychology, self-help, and leadership best practices. In other words, the primary obstacle in the promotion of the ministry of deliverance and healing within the Church is that of the worldview of her leaders. This isn't, however, to discard relevant discoveries in the fields of psychology and leadership theory. The shift is towards a worldview that can embrace both without any needed conflict.

Os Guinness supports this perspective. He vehemently argues that whereas the roots of Christianity and Judaism recognize a war against evil, seen through spiritual eyes, the current secular worldview in the Church can only address spiritual matters via humanistic means.[180] This lack of a spiritual worldview is detrimental to the work of the great commission. The Western world is increasingly open and curious about the supernatural and the paranormal, and the Church needs to catch up. As the great missionary Hudson Taylor once said,

> We are a supernatural people, born again by a supernatural birth, kept by a supernatural power, sustained on supernatural food, taught by a supernatural Teacher, from a supernatural Book. We are led by a supernatural Captain in right paths to assured victories.[181]

Since the arrival of the church growth movement of the 1980s and 1990s, much of the Church has become similar to her surrounding environs (i.e., 'seeker-sensitive'). Certainly, there were many positive outcomes with this movement, especially so of evangelistic endeavors. Consequently, however, the Church has become uncomfortable on the margins and reluctant to embrace ministry expressions that don't have a broad embrace from cultural elites. Don't forget, throughout history, the broad masses have always been more open to the supernatural during times when elitist thought wasn't open. No wonder ministries of healing and deliverance have been sequestered to the back rooms, if present at all.

Miroslav Volf argues that Christianity was meant to flourish from the margins and that "for the early Christian communities, to

---

180   Oz Guinness, *Impossible People,* Kindle edition, chapter 3.

181   Given by J. Hudson Taylor, founder of the China Inland Mission, in Carnegie Hall, NYC, April 23, 1900.

be persecuted was not a cause of alarm but an (unpleasant) occasion for rejoicing."[182] Responding to anticipated fear the Church might experience if/when she finds herself marginalized or persecuted for being different than her surroundings, Volf suggests that her very being as "different" is core to her gospel potency.

> Literally, everything depends on difference... If you have difference, you have the gospel. If you don't you will either have just plain old culture or the universal reign of God, but you won't have the gospel. The gospel is always also about difference; after all, it means the good news—something good, something new, and therefore something different.[183]

JEREMY AND ANDREA ENCOUNTER JESUS'S PEACE

My brother, Jeremy, is four years younger than me, and we are opposite in most ways, but especially in faith. And isn't it just like Jesus to use faith to bring us together? Jeremy would often mock my Christian beliefs and get angry at even hearing the name of Jesus. Yet we recently realized that we both see in the spiritual realm. While I may refer to spiritual beings as angels and demons, Jeremy would say "ghosts." We recently began to talk about what we both experienced growing up in our family home, and eventually, he was more open to hearing how I, as a Christian, operate in the spiritual realm.

This all paved the way for him calling me for help in his home, as the "friendly ghosts" that occupied their space began to turn and become more confrontational. My brother and his fiancé began to feel, hear, and see these demons operate in ways they only saw in Hollywood-produced horror films.

---

182   Miroslav Volf, *A Public Faith: How Followers of Christ Should Serve the Common Good* (Grand Rapids: Baker Publishing, 2011), 79.

183   Ibid., 95.

I had never gone into a demonized home that Christians didn't own, and I wasn't 100% sure I was comfortable getting rid of these demons (wondering if Matthew 12:45 held value here: would these demons simply leave and come back with seven more evil than itself?). I also didn't want to portray Jesus as some "genie." After much prayer and chatting with trusted mentors, I invited a friend to come out to my brother's home with me. What happened that night, I could not have expected. Jesus did more than I could have dreamt of (Eph 3:20)!

As my friend and I sat with Jeremy and his fiancé, Andrea, they shared their story. While they may believe in friendly ghosts, follow Buddhism, love horror flicks and skulls, they are also two gentle and loving individuals who were now shaking in fear. Jesus used my friend and me in different ways, and it was a beautiful affirmation as to why I was supposed to bring someone along with me. As Andrea shared a little of her story, my friend simply said, "I think there's some sadness in you." and asked if she could say a simple prayer. As my friend put her hand on Andrea, Andrea immediately burst into tears. She kept saying she didn't understand what was happening, and that she had never felt so much peace in her life. "What is this magic?" she exclaimed!

Meanwhile, I was able to break curses off my brother. As lights flickered around us while I did so, he would "name" the demon without realizing it. He followed me around the house as I either silenced or got rid of whatever demons God allowed me, and my brother sensed them all leave. I began to see how we had similar abilities to perceive the spiritual world, and the enemy was trying to hijack his ability for destructive purposes.

As Andrea fought a panic attack, I placed my hands on her, and she immediately calmed down. I later realized that my friend and I might have had some words of knowledge, but often, we simply lay our hands on them. With no words, we were merely conduits of God's love and grace. They were touched in ways I couldn't have manufactured if I tried!

This cemented a deeper bond between my brother and me, and it opened a door where I can say the name of Jesus around him. They also have peace and quiet in their home now. They may not have come to Christ yet, but they felt and experienced Jesus. It was tangible. Their story is not over!

The following is a suggested roadmap to follow in shifting towards a biblical and historical supernatural worldview.

a. Intentionally shape the Church's supernatural worldview. Given the Church's historic pattern towards unbelief, educate people of a basic kingdom/biblical/spiritual worldview. Help them see how an exclusive view of rationalism and scientific materialism fights against the Kingdom of God. Help the Church become comfortable to thrive on the margins rather than the existential-suicidal pursuit of acceptability and accommodation.

b. Demonstrate from Scripture with support from the Church Fathers that healing and deliverance are primary effects of the Kingdom of Light displacing the kingdom of darkness. In the words of Graham Twelftree,

> … the exorcisms are not… preparatory to the coming of the kingdom. They do not illustrate, extend, or even confirm Jesus's preaching. In the casting out of the demons, the mission of Jesus itself is taking place, being actualized or fulfilled. In short, *in themselves the exorcisms of Jesus are the Kingdom of God in operation* (italics his).[184]

---

[184] Graham H. Twelftree, *Jesus the Exorcist: A Contribution to the Study of the Historical Jesus* (1993, repr., Eugene, Oregon: Wipf & Stock, 2010) 170.

The *Lausanne Movement*, in its 2000 gathering in Nairobi, Kenya, supported this historical position in its statement related to spiritual warfare. "Deliverance from Satanic and demonic powers and influence in the ancient church was used as proof of the resurrection and the truth of the claims of Christ by the church fathers."[185]

c. Teach that believers can be demonized and that complete freedom from the same is found through the power, the name, and authority of Jesus Christ.

d. Demonstrate that the supernatural is meant to be a natural occurrence in the Kingdom of God. Tell stories of God's miraculous work today as they emerge. Neill Foster quotes R.C. Sproul in his book, *The Invisible Hand* (1997), "Christianity is based upon and rooted in miracles. Take away the miracles, and you take away the Christian faith. Church history, of course, is replete with attempts to do this."[186]

The *Lausanne Movement* shares this recommendation for the formation of a biblical worldview, and urgently so within theological training centers.[187]

---

[185] Lausanne Movement. *Deliver us from Evil—Consultation Statement*. Official records from Nairobi 2000 gathering, 22 August 2000, p. 5) Accessed online July 3, 2018, https://www.lausanne.org/content/statement/deliver-us-from-evil-consultation-statement.

[186] Neill K. Foster, *Sorting out the Supernatural*. Camp Hill (Pennsylvania: Christian Publications, 2001), 3.

[187] Access the full Lausanne statement here: https://www.lausanne.org/content/statement/deliver-us-from-evil-consultation-statement.

In my observation, many Christian leaders shy away from making such behavioral shifts in worldview. I don't blame them for this but rather invite them into a deeper freedom in Christ. God is an infinite being. You can't come to the end of your experience of him. There is more of his nature to be discovered. More of his presence. More of his voice. More of his freedom. More of his empowerment. And while all this is true, we can't give away what we haven't received. We can't lead others where we haven't been.[188]

PASTOR BRENT BRINGS DEEP FREEDOM

We have a lady in our church in her early sixties, one of those loyal, faithful members of the church who never missed a Sunday service or church event. A delightful addition to any church congregation. When we began a study focused on uncovering the truth about ourselves and who God is, called Soul Care, *she declined to participate, not that she was against it; she simply said she was too busy.*

As her pastor, my first instinct was that her avoidance of the Soul Care *journey meant she very much needed to participate in* Soul Care. *However, I have also learned that I often cannot change anyone's mind. I simply prayed that if she needed to go through* Soul Care, *the Holy Spirit would lead her.*

A few months later, she came to me and said, "I think I need to do Soul Care." *I arranged a meeting with a lady of her age who knew how to lead people through deliverance and inner healing. They worked through the content on their own while I helped out with inner healing and took the lead for the deliverance portion of the material.*

In a deliverance session, we "tested the spirits" (as the scriptures say) by simply asking the Holy Spirit to shine a light on any dark spirit that may be present. We command in Jesus's name that any evil spirit make its presence

---

188   This I explore more deeply in my previous book, *The Empowerment Pivot: How God is Redefining our View of Normal* (2020).

known. We then ask a series of questions that an evil spirit caught in the light of Jesus cannot answer correctly. The first question is, "Is Jesus your Lord?" I was shocked when this woman was unable to state that Jesus was Lord verbally. I had assumed this faithful church lady would sail through the test, yet an evil spirit had been uncovered.

The evil spirit stated its purpose in her was anger. Honestly, I was doubtful, at first, that this could be true because she was so incredibly sweet! When I asked if this made sense to her, she replied, "Oh yes, I've had terrible anger my whole life. I'm very good at hiding it, but my children could tell you stories."

We led her through the deliverance session dealing with a few evil spirits. We advised her to stay away from things that would lead her back into anger and prayed for her to be filled with the Holy Spirit.

A few weeks later, she reported that she was so much more at peace. The anger that always simmered just below the surface was gone. She also told us how before deliverance she always found reading scripture and praying to be boring and a chore that she forced herself to do. After her deliverance, she said she couldn't wait to read the Bible and her prayer life had come alive. Two years after her deliverance she remains a woman of incredible prayer and scripture reading, spending a few hours each day studying the Word and in prayer.

We also have the testimony of her daughter, who was skeptical about deliverance ministry, reporting a noticeable change in her mom. Her daughter said to me, "Mom is almost never angry like she used to be. She is more at peace and talks about Jesus all the time."

Without deliverance, this lady would likely have remained plateaued in her discipleship journey. Years of church attendance and bible studies had not resulted in dealing with things that blocked her from advancing in her relationship with Jesus. As she said, "I have grown more in my faith in these last two years than in the previous twenty."

Jesus said as much to his first disciples in Matthew 10:7–8. Perhaps most of us are familiar with the phrase spoken by Jesus, *"… Freely you have received; freely give"* (Matthew 10:8). Do you know what the preceding sentence is?

> *As you go, proclaim this message: 'The kingdom of heaven has come near.' Heal the sick, raise the dead, cleanse those who have leprosy, drive out demons. Freely you have received; freely give.*
> —Matthew 10:7–8

Make no mistake. Jesus is pointing out to his disciples that he has healed them, he has driven out their demons, he has brought the holistic gospel to their very lives and wildly expanded their worldview. From this point of transformation, using all you have received from me, go and do likewise.

For Christian leaders unfamiliar with the ministries of healing and deliverance, the journey before them might seem intimidating. Our current church structures frequently set up the office of the pastor as the one who is expected to know all the answers to all their questions. Those who advance in the Kingdom of God, however, choose the posture of a child. A child is eager to learn, isn't prideful about knowledge, and welcomes instruction from those who know more. A child isn't concerned about having to get things right the first time. A child intuitively embraces development.

For many reading this book, their first step may well be to invite Jesus to bring his transforming presence more deeply into their lives, in the place(s) yet-to-be-fully redeemed. Jesus planted twelve tamarisk trees in his early apostles. He still plants tamarisk trees.

CHAPTER TWELVE

DISCIPLE-MAKING, DELIVERANCE & HEALING

I will keep you and will make you to be a covenant for the people and a light for the Gentiles, to open eyes that are blind, to free captives from prison and to release from the dungeon those who sit in darkness.

—Isaiah 42:6–7

The church has only one primary mission. The mission isn't primarily to plant or build churches (didn't Jesus say that he would build his church?). The mission isn't primarily to run programs and build Christian organizations. The mission is primarily to make disciples. And not merely disciples but disciples that can reproduce disciples, doing the works that Jesus did and in his authority.

Therefore go and make disciples of all nations, baptizing them in the name of the Father and of the Son and of the Holy Spirit, and teaching them to obey everything I have commanded you. And surely I am with you always, to the very end of the age.

—Matthew 28:19–20

What did Jesus teach his followers? Certainly, he taught them to live lives of humility, generosity, and service. He taught them to stand against injustice and to defend the weak. Despite these being true and necessary, his ministry was more frequently described as proclaiming the good news of the kingdom, healing the sick, and casting out demons. These traits are the primary indicators of what disciples are intended to do.

Tragically, the ministries of healing and (especially) deliverance have largely been marginalized since Christianity was formally organized following the Constantinian era of the fourth century. Yet leading missiologists have concluded that, as the norm, healing and deliverance have accompanied the advance of the gospel when crossing cultural borders throughout history.[189] As taught by Christ and modeled in the early church, healing and deliverance must regain their rightful place—in the disciple-making processes of the church, not making too much of it nor too little.

Using the Great Commission as a framework, let's embrace the restoration of healing and deliverance ministries as critical to the disciple-making process.

HEALING & DELIVERANCE IN THE BAPTISMAL PROCESS

As we explored in Chapter 7, the early church significantly incorporated deliverance into the pre-baptismal experience, recognizing it as an early necessity in the journey of faith. So sacred were the baptismal waters that they didn't permit new converts to enter before engaging in a deliverance process. This process frequently took weeks or months as their newfound salvation was appropriated into various facets of their lives, ensuring that the kingdom of darkness was being swept clean. Through the waters of baptism, victory over darkness and the expulsion of demonic spirits were secured. Mirroring this is the story of the ancient Hebrews in their flight from Egypt, with their enemies drowning in the waters.

---

[189]   Keener, *Miracles,* 845.

Church leaders would do well to see baptism less as a metaphor and more as a vehicle for advancing experiential freedom in new believers. Care should be taken early in the disciple-making process (i.e., the first few weeks) to ensure that Jesus is given broad access to light up every area of darkness. What is needed is profound, experienced redemption coupled with orthodox, cognitive belief and empowerment by the Holy Spirit. Through this, the church will be better equipped and intrinsically motivated to be agents of redemption in every facet of society, among every ethnic group on earth.

Again, the *Lausanne Movement,* Consultative Statement from 2000 aligns with this recommendation,

> We call for churches to develop an understanding of sanctification that addresses all of the human person: our spiritual, emotional, mental, and physical selves. Such a holistic understanding of sanctification will include the development of spiritual disciplines, *inner healing*, and *deliverance*. All need to become tools supporting the sanctification of Christians through the Word by the Holy Spirit …. There is a need to explore the role in spiritual conflict of the practices of baptism, holy communion, confession of sin and absolution, foot-washing, and anointing with oil.[190] (emphasis mine)

I know of some churches that are taking baptism as a vehicle toward deliverance very deliberately. New disciples of Christ are quickly introduced to pathways that lead to profound freedom from demonic spirits and the opportunity for Jesus to heal them physically, emotionally, and relationally. Baptism is no longer viewed merely "an outward sign of an inward reality." Such

---

[190] Lausanne Movement, *Deliver us from Evil—Consultation Statement*, p. 12.

language represents a secular approach to the subject and represents the anti-miraculous movement throughout church history. Instead, water baptism (and the process leading up to it) can become a nail in the coffin to all things representing darkness in the life of a new believer. In the discipling process towards, and culminating in, water baptism, Jesus lights up their dark.

Following an intentional pre-baptism journey that isn't merely cognitive (i.e., catechism) but is also experiential, the baptismal waters can be sanctified by a simple declaration such as,

> In the name of Jesus Christ and for his glory, we sanctify these waters of baptism. We declare that all who enter these waters do so under the authority of Jesus and command all remaining evil spirits to remain buried and defeated. We sanctify these waters to be a place of victory and light to all those who emerge from these waters, filled with the Spirit of Jesus, embraced by the love of their Heavenly Father, and sent into the world as his ambassadors.

Healing and deliverance are not only for new believers. Because these have suffered such neglect for decades, church leaders shouldn't assume they can't also benefit from such ministries. Indeed, the data from my research presents a compelling picture that many negative internal realities experienced by church leaders (and laity) may in fact be a scheme of the enemy. In my previous book, *The Empowerment Pivot: How God is Redefining our View of Normal* (2020), I share numerous personal narratives of Jesus's work in my own life. These include being set free from demonic spirits and experiencing deep healing to my emotional and physical world. Additionally, I have heard hundreds, if not thousands, of such accounts from other Christian leaders.

TRAIN PRACTICALLY AND RELEASE BROADLY

The ministries of healing and deliverance have tended to veer into the ditch of neglect when sequestered to the clergy class, or the ditch of excess when held onto by a few exclusive practitioners. Jesus never sent anyone out on a mission without training them first to proclaim the gospel, heal the sick, and cast out demons. While certainly there will be individuals in the church who have these as primary expressions of an equipping ministry, everyone in the Kingdom of God can and should be participants in these ministries. Every pastor must gain some knowledge, experience, and competence to lead their congregations and equip the saints in this direction.

In the early church, such ministry was the domain of all believers. Therefore, for the contemporary church to recover its true Kingdom expression, practical training needs to be offered for and by the church so that the people of God can participate in these primary signs of Kingdom advance. As Rob Reimer states, "If the church doesn't do deliverance, who will? If the church does not own her spiritual authority, who can? If the church does not set people free in the name of Jesus, where can these souls go for help?"[191] Specifically, people need practical training and modeling. Most practitioners agree that while books are helpful, the equipping of these ministries needs hands-on observation, training, and coaching.

This training will take into consideration the various components of a successful healing and deliverance ministry. Paramount to these is the needed soul work. This spiritual foundation is necessary to defeat the enemy's grounds and thereby provide the means for natural spiritual maturity to occur, both before and after the removal of demonic spirits. This most certainly includes becoming rooted in the scriptures with an identity formed around their

---

[191] Rob Reimer, *Soul Care: 7 Transformational Principles for a Healthy Soul* (Franklin, Tennessee. Carpenter's Son Publishing, 2016, 237.

adoption as children of God. Matters such as repentance, identity in Christ, the forgiveness of others, inner healing, and other elements of Christian maturation must be seen as partners in the freedom one experiences through deliverance and healing.

Churches with little recent history in healing and deliverance might find the journey forward intimidating, especially so for its senior leaders. It may be wise for senior leadership to endorse the development of such ministries but for a time have these develop under the wing of associate or lay leaders. In some contexts, especially for larger churches, it is wise for the senior leader to not be the "face" of the ministry. There may be a need in such environments to bless and sanction a forward-exploration group while not forcing the entire congregation to embrace such experience too rapidly. For some churches to do otherwise might irrevocably cause division or loss of credibility.

We must mature the church without wrecking the church. We must move the church forward with noted speed yet slow enough to allow people carefully to "get on the bus." Associate pastors and lay leaders can be models in leading the way but need private and public support from senior leadership.

APPROACHES IN HEALING AND DELIVERANCE

Anyone exploring this topic will quickly discover that there is a range of similarities and differences to various approaches in healing and deliverance. Regrettably, and most certainly immaturely, some see this as a strong point of contention, arguing that specific methods are the "biblical" ones. Rather than this being a source of frustration, it may be helpful to recognize that the Gospels depict a different reality.

The miracles presented in the Gospels display a range of methods employed by Jesus. He spoke the miraculous into being, he rubbed mud into someone's eyes, he commanded demons to speak, he commanded demons to be silent. Seemingly, Jesus didn't have a specific method. Instead, he said what he heard his Father say and did what he saw his Father doing. The fact that such a broad methodology was demonstrated by Jesus, without any critique by the gospel writers, suggests that his methods are to be taken up by all followers of Jesus today.[192]

Notwithstanding, there are core principles that can guide us in biblical methodology on healing and deliverance.

1. Methods must represent the person of Christ well, his compassion, his grace, his sovereignty, and his kindness.

2. Methods need to employ the authority of the believer in Christ.[193]

3. Methods shouldn't be harmful, manipulative, traumatizing, or shaming towards those being ministered to and those ministering.

4. Methodological approaches are helpful in the early days of training. Over time, however, one should learn to rely upon methodology less and less while a dependence upon the Holy Spirit should increase as one matures.

5. Approaches in healing and deliverance should result in the primary attention being upon Christ rather than the demonic or the illness.

6. Methods shouldn't merely aim to remove the demonic or heal the illness or injury. Rather, the goal is to

[192] Graham H. Twelftree, "Healing and Exorcism in the Early Church," in *Healing and Exorcism in Second Temple Judaism and Early Christianity*, ed. Michael Tellbe & Tommy Wasserman, (Tubingen Germany: Mohr Siebeck, 2019), 127.

[193] An excellent resource on this topic is Chuck Davis, *The Bold Christian: Using Your God-Given Spiritual Authority as a Believer* (New York, NY: Beaufort Books, 2013).

introduce the person more deeply to the person and presence of Jesus, through the Holy Spirit. This is the end game. The fullness of Christ through his Spirit.

HEALTH, PSYCHIATRY & PSYCHOLOGY PROFESSIONALS

The research data indicates a high degree of positive effect related to matters of mental and physical wellness. (i.e., 96% of participants experienced a measure of emotional healing; 43.5% some measure of physical healing). All knowledge comes from the mind of God, even that of the scientific realm. Therefore, there is no intrinsic conflict between the fields of science and the Kingdom of God.

Church leaders would benefit by collaborating with medical and psychological professionals. Medical and psychological professionals would also benefit by partnering with Christ-followers who operate in healing and deliverance. Even better, both would benefit by adapting their capacity to integrate both natural and supernatural possibilities for healing and freedom. James Friesen, in his book, *Uncovering the Mystery of MPD (Multiple Personality Disorder)*, represents stellar efforts in this regard.

Once again, this recommendation aligns with that of the *Lausanne Movement,*

Specifically we call for:
- A sustained dialogue between those engaged in deliverance ministries and those in the medical and psychological professions.
- Urgent sharing worldwide with deliverance practitioners of the current state of knowledge of Dissociative Identity Disorder (DID), formerly called Multiple Personality Disorder.

- A diagnostic approach that allows practitioners to discern the difference between DID personalities and spiritual entities.
- A dialogue between theologians and the medical and psychological professions that develops a holistic understanding of the human person, inseparably relating body, mind, emotions, and spirit as they function individually and relationally.[194]

A PSYCHOLOGIST'S STORY OF HEALING
IN A SURVIVOR OF CHILDHOOD ABUSE

I am a Registered Psychologist in the Province of Alberta. I maintain an active counseling practice in Calgary, Alberta. I have had the honor and pleasure of working with a woman who endured repeated, severe abuse in multiple abuse domains during the very early years of her brain's development. During psychotherapy sessions, the traumatic symptoms she described were consistent with a Dissociative Identity Disorder (DID) diagnosis. The Diagnostic And Statistical Manual of Mental Disorders *explains:*

> *Dissociative identity disorder is characterized by a) the presence of two or more distinct personality states or an experience of possession and b) recurrent episodes of amnesia. The fragmentation of identity may vary with culture (e.g., possession-form presentations) and circumstance. Thus, individuals may experience discontinuities in identity and memory that may not be immediately evident to others or are obscured by attempts to hide dysfunction. Individuals with dissociative identity disorder experience a) recurrent, inexplicable intrusions into their conscious functioning and sense of self (e.g., voices dissociated actions and speech, intrusive*

---

194 Lausanne Movement. *Deliver us from Evil—Consultation Statement*, p. 12.

thoughts, emotions, and impulses), b) alterations of sense of self (e.g., attitudes, preferences, and feeling like one's body or actions are not one's own), c) odd changes of perception (e.g., depersonalization or derealization, such as feeling detached from one's body while cutting), and d) intermittent functional neurological symptoms. Stress often produces transient exacerbation of dissociative symptoms that makes them more evident."[195]

In the early part of her treatment, I assessed her: 1) physical wellness, 2) emotional wellness, 3) psychological wellness, and 4) spiritual wellness. Her responses to the first three domains suggested that psychotherapy was indeed needed. When I inquired regarding her spiritual wellness (not necessarily organized religion), she stated that she was not a church attendee but had the sense that "maybe she should be." I supported her sense and she, as always, worked diligently to find a church family. On multiple occasions I was impressed and inspired by the people and circumstances that came into her life over the years. I became convinced that we were in the presence of the supernatural as I traveled alongside her during her search for spiritual well-being.

The end treatment goal in treating DID is the integration of all the various aspects of one's personality and the establishing of their co-consciousness/no more amnesia. Unfortunately, several years of therapy did not move us satisfactorily toward this end goal, which is not uncommon with DID patients. Her high sensitivity to dissociative tendencies significantly undermined psychotherapy. When she asked that I consider accompanying her during a deliverance intervention facilitated by Doug and Teri Balzer, I was happy to offer this support. To be honest, I had never heard of a deliverance intervention prior to this, despite being a practicing Christian myself.

Meeting Doug and Teri was a pleasure, to say the least. Doug explained that Teri had the gift of discernment of spirits and would inform him of what

---

[195]   American Psychiatric Association: Diagnostic and Statistical Manual of Mental Disorders:, Fifth Edition (Arlington, VA, American Psychiatric Association, 2013, pp. 291-292.

his prayers needed to address in order to relieve my troubled patient. As I witnessed Teri discern and name the internal characterizations that tormented and terrorized my patient for more than forty years, I again sensed the presence of the supernatural. Doug's powerful prayer language was used to access Christ and his power to bring deliverance from anything of an evil nature.

The intervention ended in less than two hours. I observed her move through emotional distress in which she shed many tears, but at the end of it all, she stated: "ok, we're all on the same page now." She had been muted, mutilated, and tormented by internal voices for years, which all ceased on that day. She, who had been too severely traumatized to look me in the eye or fully finish most thoughts, was now doing both. We stood and spoke outside after the deliverance in a way that we had never achieved in all our years of therapy together.

We have followed Doug's directives regarding the prioritization of spiritual practices and to continue psychotherapeutic work. I was, and continue to be, astounded by the experience that took place three years ago. Since that time, thankfully, her tormenters have not returned. Significant integration has occurred, but there is still more psychotherapeutic work to be done. Talk therapy is so much more effective when language skills can be utilized! The two of us are so very thankful for Christ and his work, through Doug and Teri, to free a troubled soul from the bondage triggered by severe, repeated early trauma!

MAINTAIN A FOCUS ON JESUS AND NOT THE DEMONIC REALM.

As we go about making disciples that make disciples, our primary focus isn't upon illness or the demonic realm. Instead, we focus on the light and glory of Jesus. Jesus never went "demon-hunting," and nor should we. He didn't cast out every demon in first-century Palestine nor heal all its sick.

He did, however, go about doing what he saw his Father doing. Jesus proclaimed the kingdom, healed the sick, and set people in bondage free. He discipled his disciples to do the same. The ministry of deliverance isn't to instill fear of demons in the church or draw attention away from Jesus Christ.[196] In the brilliant words of Graham Twelftree, "We should pay as little attention to the demonic as is pastorally possible. Yet we should confront the demonic as much as is pastorally required."[197]

---

[196]   This conclusion also supported by the Lausanne Movement. *Deliver us from Evil— Consultation Statement.*

[197]   Twelftree, *In the Name of Jesus,* 294.

CHAPTER THIRTEEN

MYTHS OF HEALING AND DELIVERANCE

There will be no more night. They will not need the light of a lamp or the light of the sun, for the Lord God will give them light. And they will reign for ever and ever.

—Revelation 22:5

In the past eight years, I have had the privilege of being present to thousands of experiences of deliverance and healing, some with complete resolution and others partial. Most of these were within "the church." Some occurred outside the church, with people who didn't know Jesus. On the physical healing side, most of these didn't occur under my hands but under the hands of God's people who'd rarely, if ever, seen God heal. Yet, in their willingness to be trained, these folks had chosen to make the necessary shifts away from myths and towards the truth, embracing God's heart to see people healed and captives set free. The following is a "top ten" list of such myths that need to be busted for healing and deliverance to be restored as critical facets to disciple-making.

MYTH #1: WE CAN'T DO WHAT JESUS DID

Jesus said the opposite in John 14:12, *"Very truly I tell you, whoever believes in me will do the works I have been doing, and they will do even greater things than these, because I am going to the Father."* Whoever believes. That includes the old, the young, the women, the men, the brave, and the timid. *Everyone* gets to play.

What works did Jesus do? Many things. He lived a holy and compassionate life. He demonstrated kindness and generosity. He was an anointed teacher and prophet. However, the most common descriptor of his ministry was proclaiming the Kingdom of God, healing the sick, and setting captives free. Jesus trained his twelve disciples to heal, and they did. He commissioned the seventy-two to heal, and they did. He commissioned the church-being-birthed in Matthew 28 to operate in his authority. The church of the apostles and the church of the following two hundred years was characterized as people who had authority over dark spirits and authority to heal. We *can* do what Jesus did. He commands us to do what he did: to make disciples that make disciples of all nations, teaching them to also obey his commands, frequently expressed by the proclamation of the gospel, the healing of the sick, and the setting free of people captive to darkness.

MYTH #2: WE DON'T HAVE THE SAME EMPOWERMENT AS JESUS

We *do* have Jesus's empowerment for both life and ministry. He is our forerunner in every way. Jesus did nothing miraculous because he was God (he was fully God when he walked the earth, and always will be). He did miracles as a Holy Spirit-anointed human being, setting aside his divine privileges. Jesus told his fearful disciples, *"... As the Father has sent me, I am sending you"* (John 20:21). And with that he breathed on them and said, *"... Receive the Holy*

Spirit" (John 20:22). We are sent in the same way Jesus was sent and with the same empowerment. What was the extent of Jesus's empowerment? He was given the Holy Spirit by his Father *"without limit"* (Jn 3:34).

Why shouldn't we take Jesus at his word on this? The bottom line is we have the same empowerment as Jesus. We may not yet understand how to operate in his empowerment or walk in the filling of his Holy Spirit (Ephesians 5:18), and we may not yet know how to release his empowerment upon others. All of these, however, are developmental opportunities rather than permanent barriers.

Suggested resources:
Shorter: Chap. 3 & 4, *The Empowerment Pivot* by Douglas Balzer
Longer: *The Bold Christian* by Chuck Davis
In-depth: *Spiritual Authority* by Rob Reimer

MYTH #3: HEALING & DELIVERANCE COMES FULLY DEVELOPED

Like all ministry expressions in the Kingdom, none of them come "fully baked," but instead need to be developed. Jesus's disciples gained some proficiency in healing and casting out demons by imitating him. Then, on one occasion, the disciples were unable to bring freedom to a demonized boy. After Jesus set him free, they asked why they failed. Jesus replied, *"This kind can come out only by prayer"* (Mark 9:29). In other words, there is more space for us to develop, and especially so in learning to recognize the guiding voice of the Holy Spirit.

Too many people become quickly discouraged when praying for healing because they have struck out. Those who are fruitful in preaching, hospitality, mercy, teaching, and so on all started with little more than a glimmer of hope. Then they learned, over time, to function in Jesus's empowerment. They developed their Holy

Spirit-anointed capacity as they walked in deeper intimacy with Jesus. They also learned some tactical protocols and best-practice matters that helped them.

The same is true for these expressions of the Kingdom. First, we crawl, then we learn to walk, and then we learn to run. I'm no longer fearful of outcomes when I minister in healing and deliverance. Each occasion is an opportunity to lean into Jesus intimately, listen to his voice, and join him in what he is already doing to bring his blessing to others. I am continually learning from the Master how he wishes to express his life through me. Our decision is whether or not we allow the Master to train and empower us in what he has commanded us to do.

Developmental Resources

Charles Kraft, *Two Hours to Freedom: A Simple and Effective Model for Healing and Deliverance.*

Rob Reimer, *Soul Care: 7 Transformational Principles for a Healthy Soul.* Reimer regularly offers both in-person and online Soul Care conferences at https://renewalinternational.org. I (Balzer) frequently teach similar material at Soul Care conferences in partnership with my wife Teri and can be accessed at www.dougbalzer.com.

A CHURCH PLANTER FINDS FREEDOM

I wanted to change the world. Jesus had called me to start a church that would start churches! To see the lost be found! To see the gospel break into the city! To heal the sick! To set captives free!

And I did not know that I was one of the captives.

My wife and I, and a great team of others, started the church and had found great success: baptisms, conversions, leaders, giving, and a good meeting space. We even began the process of starting another church within one year. We had all the success we had wanted. Our prayers were answered.

But something was wrong. Terribly wrong. My joy was like a well run dry. I was routinely getting sick, injured, and felt a spiritual numbness that was hard to displace. It didn't make sense. I should have been overjoyed, filled with hope, and enjoy the goodness of God. Instead, I wanted to lay in bed all day.

After months of discouragement, illness, and injury, I attended a deeper life conference, exploring the goodness of Jesus. A hunger for God was ignited. I participated in another conference that drew out a deeper desire for God and exposed me to the reality that even Christians can be demonized. I saw and helped many women and men experience spiritual freedom in Jesus's name. I even led this process a few times: calling unclean spirits to reveal themselves, breaking their spiritual ground in Jesus's name, and commanding them to leave. I was overjoyed with the power of God to set captives free.

And I did not know that I was one of the captives.

Then, a few days later, after the conference, I was praying and seeking the face of Jesus as intensely as I ever had. I prayed a simple and life-altering prayer. "Jesus, reveal in me anything that stands in the way of greater intimacy with you." And I felt in the pit of my soul a bubbling up of spiritual darkness that is hard to describe. It was like a dark presence came out from a vault.

And then I knew that I was one of the captives. And that Jesus had come to set captives free.

I reached out to my friend Doug, a trusted friend and mentor, who led me through the process of deliverance. He commanded any unclean spirit to reveal itself, to communicate to me, not through me, if it had any spiritual ground. If the demon had ground, I confessed and repented of my sin or unforgiveness or lies I had believed, and then Doug commanded the unclean spirit to leave. And it did. Sometimes it resisted, and further ground needed to be broken. But Jesus always won. I experienced intense joy, greater capacity for receiving the love of God, and increased spiritual power and authority as a leader. I also no longer got discouraged, injured, or ill near pivotal moments in our church.

It took a few more sessions to get entirely free—the more I became self-aware, the more I would notice spiritual interference and reach out to friends and family who could help me walk into freedom. Jesus seems to love deliverance in community because it requires great humility for me and empowers those around me to operate in the power and presence of Jesus. I am grateful for the ministry of deliverance and have now helped over a hundred get free.

Because Jesus came to set captives free.

MYTH #4: ALWAYS PRAY, "IF IT'S GOD'S WILL...."

Jesus never prayed this way when he healed people. Nor should we. Ultimately, it is God's will that all of creation *will* be healed. However, on this side of the grave, we see this still being realized, the advancing of the Kingdom of God. I'm convinced that many people use this caveat when praying for healing out of fear that 1) what if it doesn't happen and 2) what does it say about "me" if healing doesn't occur? That I don't have enough faith? Jesus never intended us to wrestle with the question of whether healing is God's will or not. He viewed the advance of the Kingdom of God through a different lens.

Did Jesus heal everyone in first-century Palestine? No. Did he heal everyone the Father directed him to? Yes. He only did what he saw his Father doing and only said what he heard his Father saying. In his Spirit-anointed humanity and out of a place of intimacy and listening to his Father's voice, Jesus demonstrated the coming Kingdom to many, most tangibly through their broken bodies being healed. Repeatedly Jesus commanded his followers (and still does) to proclaim the gospel, heal the sick and free the captives. We never wonder if it is God's will to preach the gospel. We shouldn't wrestle with the same for healing. Instead, simply release his healing presence upon people! Leave the outcomes in Jesus's hands.

MYTH #5: WE NEED TO BEG GOD TO HEAL PEOPLE

For years my prayers for healing sounded more like I was begging God, trying to get his attention, attempting to convince him that healing someone would be a good idea. I have never seen someone healed in this manner. More tragically, my prayers made me appear more compassionate than God. Ouch! Jesus didn't give us specific prayers to pray but rather his healing presence to release. Peter healed a lame man in Acts, and he didn't beg God, he simply released the healing presence of Jesus: *"... Silver or gold I do not have but what I do have I give you. In the name of Jesus Christ of Nazareth, walk"* (Acts 3:6). Because Peter possessed the Spirit of Jesus, he also possessed the healing power of Jesus. This was meant to be given away to others. In the words of the Canadian Blood Service, *It's in You to Give.*

I no longer beg God to heal people. But I do give away his healing presence. My prayers are simple yet pointed, "In Jesus name may his healing presence be released upon this illness or injury. I rebuke pain and command it to dissolve away. I command this illness or injury to come under Christ's restorative presence and for all to come into his perfect alignment. May this person know that God loves them and that even their physical body matters to him."

It's also interesting to note that in the Gospels and Acts, healing prayer is typically in the form of spoken declaration and command rather than petition (asking). "Be healed." "Rise and walk." These are prayers of releasing the Kingdom of God. As Christ-followers, we have far more to give away than we know.

MYTH #6: DEMONS ARE BEHIND EVERY BUSH!

If all you have is a hammer, everything looks like a nail. If all a person knows is deliverance, then every problem will be seen as demonic. This is harmful, and this myth too often leads to manipulation and abuse. Not everything has a demonic root. Forty percent of Jesus's healing involved the demonic in some manner. This tells us two things. One, overt demonic activity is not behind most ailments. In a majority of cases, they are purely physiological or psychological. In those cases, they should be treated as such.

However, forty percent is no small number, so we shouldn't be surprised that some matters have a demonic root. Our role, as the people of God, is to be discerning. We can test the spirits. We can listen to the voice of the Holy Spirit to give us direction. We can partner with medical practitioners to not overstep into areas where we don't have expertise.

MYTH #7: IF AT FIRST YOU DON'T SUCCEED, GIVE UP!

For years I prayed for people; that is, I would pray *once* for people. If nothing ever happened (and it never did), I would give up, thinking that it wasn't God's will. Jesus didn't operate this way. Many of his healings occurred immediately, but in Mark 8 we see a story of Jesus needing to release healing more than once. After making mud with his saliva and some dirt, the blind man's sight wasn't fully healed. Jesus then *checked in* with him, "Do you see anything?" The man had received partial healing that wasn't complete in round one. He needed round two. If Jesus needed to pray more than once for someone, indeed, we have permission to pray multiple times!

One of the most significant areas of breakthrough in my ministry, and hundreds of others I have seen, is this matter of persisting in prayer. Frequently there is some sort of blockage that can often be discerned by asking, "Holy Spirit, is there anything that might be blocking what you wish to do in this person's life today?" Then listen. If the person being prayed for is a believer, invite them to listen to Jesus's whispers. There may be nothing. But there may be some forgiveness that needs to be extended, a lie that needs to be renounced, the truth of the love of God for them that needs to be embraced, and so on.

It's my observation that most healings for non-believers are primarily an invitation to salvation. There is typically little "soul work" that needs to be done. For believers, however, healing is usually an invitation to deeper sanctification as well. God desires to bless people's entire being. When praying for people for healing, watch for this deeper dynamic.

When praying for people, it can be helpful to check in with them every couple of minutes. Some questions can be helpful. "How are you doing?" "Do you sense anything going on in your body or soul?" "If the pain (or effect of the illness) was ranked a ten when we started to pray, and we are going for a zero, what number are you now at?" Any increased pain during prayer for healing almost always betrays demonic involvement. With forty percent of Jesus's healings involved some form of demonic activity, don't be surprised by this.

Many of the healings I have witnessed involved praying up to two, four, or even ten times! Whatever you do, don't give up until one of two things happens. One, the healing effect is realized. Yet, there are times when one may not see this (not everyone I pray for is healed). Second, the effectiveness of some prayer for healing is impossible to know in the moment. Some medical conditions require further testing for confirmation. Therefore, another reason to stop praying is when those ministering have a sense that they have fully cooperated with the Spirit in that moment. Just don't give up too soon!

MYTH #8: DELIVERANCE NEEDS TO BE DRAMATIC

I have come across many people hesitant towards deliverance because of what they have seen in the past. Their experience has been negatively marked by episodes of people yelling, matters getting out of control, highly demonstrative manifestations of a demonic presence, and so forth.

Yelling betrays approaches to deliverance that do not reside in the authority of Christ. Effective deliverance isn't the result of increased vocal volume. Deliverance is effective because it bears the authority and presence of Jesus. High drama is not needed. Occasionally I take great pleasure in casting demons out with a whisper as it keenly demonstrates the absolute authority Jesus has. At times a heightened demonic manifestation might be seen, but this can be controlled and does not need to get out of hand. I have done numerous deliverances in coffee shops with other customers completely unaware! On one occasion, I had a conversation with a pastor who was deeply discouraged, and he suspected he had made an agreement with the enemy's lies of condemnation. After he renounced these agreements (renouncing the grounds) and stated a verbal embrace of his identity in Christ, the statement to expel the demonic forces was simple and spoken in a quiet voice. "In Jesus name, I declare that you, spirit of discouragement, are defeated. I command you to leave this man and go where Jesus sends you." It left, and Jesus set this man free from persistent condemning thoughts.

The bottom line is that Jesus loves to honor people and restore their dignity. Whatever approach we use must reflect his love for all people and avoid every perception of abuse, manipulation, and grandstanding.

MYTH #9: NO HEALING? CONDEMN THE PERSON

I am so repulsed when I hear stories of Christians condemning others when healing does not occur. After my infant daughter's death, someone told me that her death was my fault, that she had died because of my sin. The Holy Spirit does bring conviction where necessary but only to bring a person to repentance and not towards condemnation.

I suspect those who condemn others in prayer are wrestling with their own insecurities. When answered prayer doesn't happen, they resort to blaming. The truth is, they can't heal people. We can't either. Only Jesus can heal. Our part is to walk intimately with him, extend his restorative presence, and give his blessing away to others. Not everyone I pray for receives healing. I have also not developed a robust theology as to "why God doesn't heal." It is not apparent to me that God provides such to us in the scriptures. When healing isn't realized, our aim should be to reflect the heart of that person's Heavenly Father. He loves them. They matter to him. They are precious to him. Instead of condemning or even getting stuck in the ditch of trying to "explain why God didn't heal," simply bless them. Out loud. In Jesus's name. Assure them of God's love.

MYTH #10: HEALING: ONLY FOR CHRISTIANS

In his book, *Anointed for Business,* Ed Silvoso notes that of the forty observable miracles in the Book of Acts, thirty-nine of them occurred outside religious environments. This statistic ought to wake the church up to look outside. Indeed, the heart of God is toward those who are sick in the church; James 5 is evidence of that. Yet, disproportionately, the heart of our Shepherd is towards those who haven't yet tasted and seen that God is good, the one lost sheep. In a world where skepticism surrounding Christianity is high, the front door to faith may not be a cognitive, gospel message or argument, but a divine encounter with God's love, experienced in their body or soul.

I have learned that Jesus is highly desirous to show his love to people via healing, touching those who might otherwise not have a random thought towards him. When Jesus gives me a quiet prompting to pray for the healing of a not-yet-believer or to simply release God's peace upon them, I have learned not to hesitate. There is more grace in these situations than in *any other environment I have encountered!*

I dare anyone reading this book to ask Jesus to give them a personalized, right-sized assignment of releasing his transforming presence to someone who isn't yet a part of his Kingdom. Then wait and listen for his promptings and respond obediently. It may happen in the next moment or in the next week. But it will happen! Invite him to develop his ministry uniquely through your life. The divine demonstration of the gospel, proceeding its proclamation, may very well be one of the greatest opportunities for the church to realize the Kingdom of God in the post-Christendom West. Jesus lights up the dark!

EVENTS AND TRAINING RESOURCES
IN HEALING & DELIVERANCE

www.dougbalzer.com
https://renewalinternational.org
www.heartssetfree.org

INFO-GATHERING IN DELIVERANCE

Deliverance requires information about whether evil spirits are present, if they have grounds, if these grounds have been removed, and if demons have departed. Critical to this information gathering is determining the root(s) of the problem.

Take a stomach ache, for example. The root cause could be physiological, psychological, or spiritual. If physiological, perhaps the pizza eaten the night before had turned sour. Call the doctor. If psychological, perhaps worry and anxiety has left them with stomach problems. Call the therapist. If spiritual, perhaps the enemy has gained access and is causing torment in their life. Call the deliverance team. The deliverance practitioner must hold all these possibilities in mind and not extend beyond their area of experience.

Within this arena of information gathering, I have developed a framework whereby there are three ways to gather information pertaining to demonization.

THE DIRECT APPROACH

In the direct approach, the deliverance practitioner speaks directly to the demons present. The person being ministered to reports what they hear, see, or feel. It should be noted that questions are stated that demand a yes/no response, or require an answer in a single word or phrase. I never allow demons to speak freely or at length. The strength of this approach is that it is easy to teach, provides compelling evidence when skeptics observe, and is a straightforward way to *"test the spirits,"* as urged in 1 John 4:1.

The limitation of this approach is that demons tend to lie. However, they can be compelled to speak the truth relatively easily. The process can be slow, and the focus is somewhat more upon the demonic. Regardless, Jesus functioned in this way (he conversed with demons),[198] and therefore his followers have the freedom to do so.

THE DEMONSTRATIVE APPROACH

In the demonstrative approach, the practitioner merely observes what is being demonstrated before them. Physical and verbal manifestations aren't uncommon. Sudden shaking, for example, is often a spirit of fear. A deep sigh with a suddenly relaxed body is frequently a manifestation of the presence of Jesus being received. What has been demonstrated and observed forms the basis for gathered information.

The strength of this approach is that it is highly accessible to people with little training and doesn't require a highly tuned gift of discernment or discernment of spirits. Its limitation is that it doesn't readily reveal legal grounds for demons to be present and doesn't supply an adequate spiritual test. Yet, again, Jesus functioned in this, and therefore his followers have the freedom to do so as well. A helpful hint: keep your eyes open when ministering to people or you will miss much of this.

---

198   Mark 5:1-13

THE DISCERNMENT APPROACH

In the discernment approach, the source of information is the Holy Spirit. He provides what is needed to the deliverance team through prompted thought, sight, perception, or emotion. Strengths of this approach include the brilliant focus upon Christ and his Spirit and the marvelous strategic knowledge that they share. As such, deliverance utilizing this approach tends to move much more quickly than other approaches. All Christ-followers have a measure of discernment that can be developed over time which can be most useful in this approach. Additionally, some have a gift of discernment of spirits,[199] whose ministry may be more frequently associated with deliverance.

This approach, however, also has limitations. The discerner needs to be developed over time, as with all spiritual gifts. As such, this approach is less accessible within faith communities that are new to deliverance. It is more challenging to teach quickly and doesn't provide a classical test, demanding the spirit present to proclaim, *"Jesus is Lord"* (1 Corinthians 12:3).

In this approach as well, Jesus functioned and much more frequently. Although Christ-followers have the freedom to utilize all three approaches, the maturing person will, over time, increasingly use the discernment approach. This is a natural result of walking more deeply in intimacy with Jesus, attentive to the voice of Holy Spirit.

---

[199] 1 Cor 12:10

INFO-GATHERING IN DELIVERANCE: 3 APPROACHES

Approach	Source of Information	Strengths	Limitations	Note
Direct	Demons: speaking directly to	-Easier to teach -Apologetic to sceptics -Ability to 'test the spirits' (1 Jn 4:1)	-Demons lie -Focus upon demonic -Can be slow	Jesus did this (Mk 5:9, 1 Cor. 12:3)
Demonstrative	Observation of what is being demonstrated	-Accessible -Does not require high discernment	-Not likely to reveal root or grounds -Does not 'test'	Jesus did this (Mk 5:1-21)
Discernment	Holy Spirit	-Focus more on God -Strat. knowledge	-Difficult to teach -Does not 'test'	Jesus did this (Mk 7:29, 1 Cor. 12:10)

MIRACLES IN THE GOSPELS

Excluding the incarnation, transfiguration and resurrection of Jesus

#	Event	Mark	Matt.	Luke	John	Category	Method
1	Man with unclean spirit	1:21-28★		4:33-36★		exorcism	command
2	Simon's mother-in-law	1:29-32	8:14-15	4:38-39		healing	touch/ command
3	Summary of many	1:32-34★	8:16-17★	4:40-41★		healing/ exorcism	touch/ command
4	Summary of many	1:39★				exorcism	
5	Cleanses a leper	1:40-44	8:2-4	5:12-15		healing	touch/ command
6	Healing of paralytic	2:2-12	9:1-8	5:17-26		healing	declaration
7	Man with withered hand	3:1-5	12:9-13	6:6-11		healing	declaration
8	Summary of many	3:10-11★				healing/ exorcism	
9	Calms a storm	4:35-41	8:23-27	8:22-25		command nature	command
10	Geresene demoniac	5:1-20★	8:28-34★	8:26-39★		exorcism	command
11	Jarius' daughter	5:21-43	9:18-25	8:40-54		resurrection	command
12	Bleeding woman	5:24-34		8:43-48		healing	touch
13	Summary of many	6:5	13:58			healing	

#	Event	Mark	Matt.	Luke	John	Category	Method
14	Summary of many	6:12★				exorcism/ healing	disciples
15	Feeds five thousand	6:30-44	14:13-21	9:10-17	6:2-14	command nature	blessing
16	Walks on water	6:45-52	14:22-31		6:16-20	command nature	
17	Wind ceasing	6:45-52	14:32-33		6:21	command nature	
18	Summary	6:53-56	14:34-36			healing	touch
19	Syrophoenician daughter	7:24-30★	15:21-28★			exorcism	declaration
20	Deaf man	7:31-37				healing	command
21	Feeds four thousand	8:1-10	15:32-39			command nature	blessing
22	Blind man at Bethsaida	8:22-26				healing	touch / spit
23	Boy with unclean spirit	9:14-29★	17:14-21★	9:38-43★		exorcism/ healing	command
24	Blind Bartimaeus	10:46-52	20:29-34	18:35-43		healing	declaration
25	Withered fig tree	11:20-25	21:18-22			command nature	declaration
26	Summary of many		4:23-25★	6:17-18★		healing/ exorcism	touch/ declaration
27	Centurion's servant		8:5-13	7:2-10		healing	declaration
28	Two blind men		9:27-31			healing	touch/ declaration
29	Man with mute spirit		9:32-34★			exorcism	command
30	Summary of many		9:35★			healing/ exorcism	
31	Summary of many		11:4-5	7:21★		healing/ exorcism	
32	Blind & mute demoniac		12:22★	11:14★		exorcism/ healing	
33	Summary of many	14:14		9:11		healing	
34	Summary of many		15:29-31			healing	
35	Summary of many		21:14			healing	
36	Large catch of fish			4:1-11		command nature	declaration

#	Event	Mark	Matt.	Luke	John	Category	Method
37	Widow's son			7:11-17		resurrection	touch/command
38	Mary Magdalene/others			8:2*		healing/exorcism	
39	Report of the 72			10:17-19*		exorcism	command
40	Woman - disabling spirit			13:11-13*		healing/exorcism	declaration
41	Various persons			13:32*		healing/exorcism	
42	Man with dropsy			14:2-4		healing	
43	Ten lepers			17:11-19		healing	declaration
44	High priest servant's ear			22:51		healing	touch
45	Jesus' resurr. appearing			24:36-49	20:19-22	command nature	
46	Water into wine				2:1-11	command nature	command
47	Official's son				4:46-54	healing	declaration
48	Invalid man				5:2-9	healing	declaration
49	Summary of many				6:2	healing	
50	Man born blind				9:1-7	healing	touch/command
51	Lazarus resurrection				11:1-44	resurrection	command
52	Large catch of fish				21:5-8	command nature	command

Exorcisms/
Accounts   8/26   8/27   11/28   0/11

★ = reference to exorcism

STATISTICS

- 52 Total miracle stories (not incl. incarnation, transfiguration and resurrection of Christ)
- 42 Stories and summaries of healing, deliverance, resurrection—81% of total
- 10 Accounts of miraculous command of nature
- 3 Resurrections
- 29 Stories of healing—not including summaries
- 13 Summary accounts of miraculous activity
- 17 Accounts of exorcism including summaries
- 33% of total miraculous accounts
- 40% of all healing/exorcism accounts
- 10 Stories of exorcism—not including summaries
- 34% of all healing/exorcism stories
- 92 Miraculous accounts—combination of all gospel writers
- Exorcism 29% of all miraculous accounts - 27/92

BIBLIOGRAPHY

Addison, Steve. *Movements that Change the World*. Smyrna, DE: Missional Press, 2009.

Alexander, Paul. *Signs and Wonders: Why Pentecostalism is the World's Fastest Growing Faith*. San Francisco: Jossey-Bass, 2009.

Amorth, Gabriele. *An Exorcist Tells His Story*. San Francisco: Ignatius Press: 1999.

Anderson, Neil T. *The Bondage Breaker*. Eugene, Oregon: Harvest House Publishers, 1990.

Ashbrook, Thomas R. *Mansions of the Heart: Exploring the Seven Stages of Spiritual Growth*. San Francisco: Jossey-Bass, 2009.

Balzer, Douglas A. "The Effect of Deliverance on the Well-Being of Christian Leaders" Doctoral dissertation, Alliance Theological Seminary, New York, 2018.

Balzer, Douglas A. *The Empowerment Pivot: How God is Redefining Our View of Normal*. Winnipeg: Word Alive Press, 2020.

Betty, Stafford. "The Growing Evidence for 'Demon Possession': What Should Psychiatry's Response be?" *Journal of Religion and Health*, Vol. 44, No. 1, Spring 2005.

Breen, Mike and Cochram, Steve. *Building a Discipling Culture: How to release a missional movement by discipling a missional movement by discipling people like Jesus did.* Pawleys Island, SC.: 3 Dimension Ministries, 2011.

Brown, Peter. *The World in Late Antiquity: AD 150-750.* London: Thames & Hudson, 1971.

Bubeck, Mark I. *Overcoming the Adversary: Warfare Praying Against the Demon Activity.* Chicago: Moody Press, 1984.

Burton, Tara Isabella. *Strange Rites: New Religions for a Godless World.* New York: PublicAffairs, 2020.

Collins, James M. *Exorcism and Deliverance Ministry in the Twentieth Century.* Eugene, Oregon: Wipf and Stock, 2009.

Cotter, Wendy. *Miracles in Greco-Roman Antiquity*, London: Routledge, 1999..

Darling, Frank C. *Biblical Healing: Hebrew and Christian Roots*, Boulder, Colorado: Vista Publications, 1989.

Daunton-Fear, Andrew. *Healing in the Early Church: The Church's Ministry of Healing and Exorcism from the First to the Fifth Century.* Eugene, Oregon: Wipf and Stock, 2009.

Davis, Chuck. *The Bold Christian: Using Your God-Given Spiritual Authority as a Believer.* New York, NY: Beaufort Books, 2013.

DeSilva, Dawna and Liebscher, Teresa. *Sozo: Saved, Healed, Delivered.* Shippensburg, PA: Destiny Image Publishers, 2016.

Dickason, C. Fred. *Demon Possession & the Christian.* Chicago: Moody Press, 1987.

du Toit, A.B. "Life in Obedience to the Torah: Jewish Belief, Worship, and Everyday Religion in the First Century AD," in *The New Testament Milieu*, ed. A.B. du Toit, vol. 2, Guide to the New Testament. Halfway House: Orion Publishers, 1998.

Eberhard, Arnold. *The Early Christians in Their Own Words.* Walden, NY: Plough Publishing House, 1997.

Ferguson, Everett. *Demonology of the Early Christian World*. Lewiston, New York: Edwin Mellon Press, 1984.

Friesen, James G. *Uncovering the Mystery of MPD (Multiple Personality Disorder)*. Eugene, Oregon: Wipf and Stock Publishers, 1997.

Foster, Neill K. *Sorting out the Supernatural*. Camp Hill, Pennsylvania: Christian Publications, 2001.

Georges, Jayson. *The 3D Gospel: Ministry in Guilt, Shame, and Fear Cultures*. Middletown, DE: Time Press, 2016.

Guinness, Os. *Impossible People: Christian Courage and the Struggle for the Soul of Civilization*. Downers Grove, Illinois: IVP Press, 2016.

Hamm, Dennis. *The Ministry of Deliverance and the Biblical Data* (1980), quoted in Francis MacNutt, *Deliverance from Evil Spirits*. Grand Rapids: Baker Publishing, 2009.

Hammond, Frank and Ida Mae. *Pigs in the Parlor: A Practical Guide to Deliverance*. 1973. Reprint, Kirkwood, MO: Impact Books, 1973, 2010.

Hill, Annette. *Paranormal Media: Audiences, Spirits and Magic in Popular Culture*. New York: Routledge, 2011.

Hull, Bill. *Conversion and Discipleship: You can't have one without the other*. Grand Rapids: Zondervan, 2016.

Jenkins, Philip. *The Next Christendom: The Coming of Global Christianity, 3rd Edition*. Oxford Press, 2011.

Jennings, Daniel R. *The Supernatural Occurrences of John Wesley*. Self-published, Sean Multimedia, 2012.

Kee, Howard Clark. *Medicine, Miracle and Magic in New Testament Times*. Cambridge: Cambridge University Press, 1986.

Keener, Craig S. *Miracles: The Credibility of the New Testament Accounts*. 2 vols. Grand Rapids, MI: Baker Academic Press, 2011.

Kelly, J.N.D. *Early Christian Doctrines*. New York: Harper and Row, 1978.

Kelsey, Morton T. *Healing and Christianity in Ancient Thought and Modern Times*. New York: Harper & Row, 1973.

Kendall, R.T. *Holy Fire*. Lake Mary, Florida: Charisma House, 2012.

King, Paul L. *Genuine Gold: The Cautiously Charismatic Story of the Early Christian and Missionary Alliance,* Tulsa, Oklahoma: Word & Spirit Press, 2006.

Koch, Kurt E. *Demonology Past and Present: Identifying and Overcoming Demonic Strongholds*. Grand Rapids, Michigan: Kregel Publications, 1973.

Kraft, Charles H. *Deep Wounds Deep Healing*. Minneapolis, Minnesota: Chosen Books, 2010.

_____. *Defeating Dark Angels: Breaking Demonic Oppression in the Believer's Life*. 1992. Reprint, Grand Rapids: Baker Publishing, 2011.

_____. *I Give You Authority: Practicing the Authority Jesus Gave us*. Minneapolis, Minnesota: Chosen Books, 2012.

_____. *The Evangelical's Guide to Spiritual Warfare*. Minneapolis, Minnesota: Chosen Books, 2015.

_____. *Two Hours to Freedom: A Simple and Effective Model for Healing and Deliverance*. Grand Rapids, Michigan: Chosen Books, 2010.

Laski, Marghanita. *Ecstasy in Secular and Religious Experience*. London: Cresset Press, 1961.

Lausanne Movement. *Deliver us from Evil—Consultation Statement*. Official records from Nairobi 2000 gathering, 22 August 2000. Accessed online July 3, 2018, https://www.lausanne.org/content/statement/deliver-us-from-evil-consultation-statement.

Leeper, Elizabeth. "From Alexandria to Rome: The Valentinian Connection to the Incorporation of Exorcism as a Prebaptismal Rite." *Vigiliae Christianae,* 44, 1990.

Liardon, Roberts, *God's Generals: Why They Succeeded and Why Some Failed*. New Kensington, Pennsylvania: Whitaker House, 1996.

_____. *God's Generals: The Healing Evangelists*. New Kensington, Pennsylvania: Whitaker House, 2011.

Lingenfelter, Sherwood G. *Leading Cross-Culturally: Covenant Relationships for Effective Christian Leadership*. Grand Rapids, Michigan: Baker Academic, 2008.

MacCasland, S.V. *By the Finger of God: Demon Possession and Exorcism in Early Christianity in Light of Modern Views of Mental Illness*. New York: Macmillian, 1951.

MacMillan, John A. *Encounter with Darkness*. 1949; *Modern Demon Possession*; repr., Harrisburg, PA: Christian Publications, 1980.

_____. *The Authority of the Believer*. Repr., Memphis: Bottom of the Hill Publishing, 1980.

MacMullen, Ramsay. *Christianizing the Roman Empire (A.D. 100-400)*. New Haven: Yale University Press, 1984.

MacNutt, Francis. *Deliverance from Evil Spirits: A Practical Manual*. Grand Rapids: Baker Book House, 1995.

Martin, Malachi. *Hostage to the Devil: The Possession and Exorcism of Five Americans*. San Francisco: Harper, 1976, 1992.

McConnell, C Douglas (editor). "The Holy Spirit and Mission Dynamics." *Evangelical Missiological Society Series,* no. 5 (1997). Pasadena: William Carey Library.

Midelfort, H. C. Erik. *Exorcism and Enlightenment: Johann Joseph Gassner and the Demons of Eighteenth-Century Germany*. New Haven, Connecticut: Yale University Press, 2005.

Miller, Donald E., Sargeant, Kimon H., Flory, Richard, eds. *Spirit and Power: The Growth and Global Impact of Pentecostalism*. New York: Oxford Press, 2013.

Muchembled, Robert. *A History of the Devil: From the Middle Ages to the Present*. Cambridge, UK: Polity Press, 2003.

Nauman, Elmo. *Exorcism Through the Ages.* New York: Philosophical Library, 1974.

Nischan, Bodo. "The Exorcism Controversy and Baptism in the Late Reformation." *The Sixteenth Century Journal*, Vol. 18, No. 1, Spring 1987.

Ogden, Greg. *Transforming Discipleship: Making Disciples a Few at a Time.* Downers Grove, IL: InterVarsity Press, 2003.

Peck, Scott M. *People of the Lie: The Hope for Healing Human Evil.* New York: Simon and Schuster, 1983.

Penn-Lewis, Jessie. *War on the Saints.* 1916. Reprint, Fort Washington, Pennsylvania: Christian Literature Crusade, 1995.

Plueddemann, James E. *Leading Across Cultures: Effective Ministry and Mission in the Global Church.* Downers Grove, Illinois: IVP Academic Press, 2009.

Porterfield, Amanda. *Healing in the History of Christianity.* New York: Oxford University Press, 2005.

Prince, Derek. *They Shall Expel Demons: What you need to know about demons—your invisible enemies.* Grand Rapids: Baker Book House, 1998.

Reimer, Rob. *Soul Care: 7 Transformational Principles for a Healthy Soul.* Franklin, Tennessee. Carpenter's Son Publishing, 2016.

Reimer, Rob. *Spiritual Authority: Partnering with God to Release the Kingdom.* Franklin, Tennessee: Carpenter's Son Publishing, 2020.

Richards, John. *But Deliver Us from Evil: An Introduction to the Demonic Dimension in Pastoral Care.* New York: Seabury Press, 1974.

Sandford, John & Mark. *A Comprehensive Guide to Deliverance and Inner Healing.* Grand Rapids, Michigan: Chosen Books, 1992.

Shaw, Jane. *Miracles in Enlightenment England.* New Haven, Connecticut: Yale University Press, 2006.

Stafford, Betty. "The Growing Evidence for 'Demon Possession': What Should Psychiatry's Response be?" *Journal of Religion and Health*, Vol. 44, No. 1, Spring 2005.

Stiller, Brian C. *From Jerusalem to Timbuktu: A World Tour of the Spread of Christianity.* Downers Grove, Illinois: IVP Books, 2018.

Swindoll, Charles R. *Demonism: How to Win Against the Devil.* Portland: Multnomah Press, 1981.

Twelftree, Graham H. *In the Name of Jesus—Exorcism among Early Christians.* Grand Rapids: Baker Academic Press, 2007.

_____. *Jesus the Exorcist: A Contribution to the Study of the Historical Jesus.* Eugene, Oregon: Wipf & Stock, 1993, 2010.

Unger, Merrill F., *Demonology in the World Today: a Study of Occultism in the Light of God's Word.* Carol Stream, Illinois: Tyndale House, 1971.

Van De Walle, Bernie A. *The Heart of the Gospel: A.B. Simpson, the Fourfold Gospel, and Late Nineteenth-Century Evangelical Theology.* Eugene, Oregon: Wipf and Stock, 2009.

Volf, Miroslav. *A Public Faith: How Followers of Christ Should Serve the Common Good.* Grand Rapids: Baker Publishing, 2011.

Wagner, C. Peter. *Spiritual Warfare Strategy: Confronting Spiritual Powers.* Shippensburg, PA: Destiny Image Publishers, 1996.

_____, ed. *Engaging the Enemy: How to Fight and Defeat Territorial Spirits.* Ventura, CA: Regal, 1993.

_____, *Wrestling with Alligators, Prophets and Theologians: Lessons from a Lifetime in the Church—a Memoir.* Ventura, CA: Regal, 2010.

Wagner, Doris M. *How to Cast out Demons: A Guide to the Basics.* Ventura, California: Regal Books: 2000.

Walton, John H. *The Lost World of Genesis One.* Downers Grove, Ill.: IVP Academic, 2009.

Webster, Robert. *Methodism and the Miraculous: John Wesley's Idea of the Supernatural and the Identification of Methodists in the Eighteenth-Century*. Lexington, Kentucky: Emeth Press, 2013.

Witherington, Ben. *The Problem with Evangelical Theology: Testing the Exegetical Foundations of Calvinism, Dispensationalism and Wesleyanism*. Waco: Baylor University Press, 2005.

Witmer, Amanda. *Jesus, the Galilean Exorcist: His Exorcisms in Social and Political Context*. Edited by Robert L. Webb and Mark Allan Powell. Vol. 10, *Library of the Historical Jesus Studies*. New York: Bloomsbury, 2012.

Wolffe, Charles, ed., *Rite of Exorcism: 1999 Rite in Latin and English*. Catholic Church: 2017.

ABOUT THE AUTHOR

Douglas A. Balzer is a catalyst for spiritual renewal. He is the Director of reKindle.tv, an organization devoted to strengthening the church towards spiritual renewal, disciple-making, and mission. As an ordained minister of The Christian and Missionary Alliance, he and his wife Teri have led more than sixty spiritual renewal retreats across Canada and in six countries. Doug earned an M.A. in Leadership and Ministry from Ambrose Seminary (Calgary) and a Doctor of Ministry from Alliance Theological Seminary at Nyack College (New York). His doctoral project, "The Perceived Effect of Deliverance on the Well-Being of Christian Leaders" won the 2019 Doctor of Ministry Dissertation Award at ATS. He is host to the reKindle podcast, is a sessional lecturer at Ambrose University, and is the author of *The Empowerment Pivot: How God is Redefining Our View of Normal*. Doug and Teri live in Calgary, Canada and have two adult sons.

www.dougbalzer.com

What if I told you that God has a version of *normal* for your life that far exceeds your current experience? What if I told you that Jesus really meant it when he said, *"Whoever believes in me will do the works I have been doing"* (John 14:12)? What if I told you that the church was meant to convincingly demonstrate Jesus's supernatural presence to a skeptical world?

This book invites you to make seven shifts towards God's eternal and infinite nature that render his manifest presence and empowerment in our lives and ministries... God's version of normal. Will you dare to pivot towards Jesus and his version of normal for your life?

www.dougbalzer.com

reKindle Renewal Podcast

The reKindle Renewal Podcast is an exploration of common themes experienced by churches and leaders in their pursuit of the renewing presence of Christ. How can the church experience renewal through the Holy Spirit and do so without wrecking the church? Hosted by Doug Balzer, this podcast includes interviews of renewal leaders and discussions about key topics and matters of equipping. Consider it an intimate backstage pass to some of the current conversations on this broad topic.

A free, online video resource!

Embark on an adventure of discovering more of the Father's love, friendship, and intimacy with Jesus, and the powerful presence and work of the Holy Spirit. No matter who you are or where you have come from, there is more of God's goodness to be discovered. This is a journey you can pursue by yourself or in a small group. Topics include growing in expectancy, removing roadblocks to the Holy Spirit, hearing God's voice, the filling of the Holy Spirit and ministering in healing. By the time you have completed this experience, you will be more deeply in love with Jesus, more fully experiencing the work of the Holy Spirit, and better equipped to be on mission with the Father, releasing his kingdom here on Earth as it is in heaven.

www.dougbalzer.com

CPSIA information can be obtained
at www.ICGtesting.com
Printed in the USA
BVHW041400221121
622233BV00014B/694

9 781486 621842